Adultery: The Forgivable Sin

Adultery:
The Forgivable Sin

Bonnie Eaker Weil, Ph.D.

with Ruth Winter, MS

Hastings House
Book Publishers
Mamaroneck, N.Y.

Library of Congress Catalog Number 94-076963

ISBN 0-8038-9364-7

This edition is published by arrangement with Carol Communications, Inc.

Printed in the United States of America

10 9 8 7 6 5 4 3

I dedicate this book to my loving parents, Hyman and Paula Eaker, of whom I am so proud. Their love and courage and belief in me made this book possible.

And to my wonderful husband, Dr. Jeffrey M. Weil, whose love I treasure.

To all the children hiding under the covers, this book is for you.

To err is human, to forgive divine.
—Alexander Pope

Contents

Foreword

We live in a difficult age for intimate relationships. Marriages break up at a rate of 40 to 50 percent, and adultery rates are over-the-top. The single-parent family is the all too common result.

Dr. Eaker Weil's book provides a service by underscoring just what adultery is all about. Adultery has a devastating impact on the entire family system. The emotional damage wrought by this betrayal of trust can hardly be assuaged by a simple "I'm sorry." It is a complex emotional issue and requires that a real sense of remorse be felt before the pattern can be broken. The hurt to husbands, wives, children, and even to later generations, runs very deep; its wounds are long lasting. *Indeed, the legacy of adultery may affect those not even born at the time of the affair.* Although the mechanism of these generational patterns is not very clear, we do know that they occur.

This book demonstrates many of the above ideas. If one agrees with these ideas, the book will enlarge and clarify them. If one does not agree, it will stimulate thought and discussion.

It is, most of all, a practical book that contains both

fascinating case histories and helpful advice. In exploring the issues of the emptiness felt by adulterers, the distance-and-pursuit phenomena in relationships, the tools of forgiveness, and how to move from self-pity toward generosity toward others, it takes on the problems of adultery in a very real and meaningful way and *proves that it is, no longer, the unforgivable sin.* It is a book that should be enormously enlightening and helpful to anyone seeking to mend a marriage or relationship.

Adultery never happens to one person. It is a systemic event which, if unexamined, will continue to wreak havoc on later generations. If it is a sin, that is why it is sinful.

Thomas F. Fogarty, M.D.
Associate Director, Emeritus
The Center for Family Learning
Ryebrook, New York

Acknowledgments

My first acknowledgment is to my devoted husband, without whose time, patience, and never-ending encouragement (even with frequent 1:00 A.M. dinners and deadlines), this book would not have been completed. I am deeply grateful for your understanding, love, and loyalty to me and my dream.

My second acknowledgment is to my mother-in-love (my mother-in-law), Helen Weil, for her invaluable and selfless contributions and dedication for giving up vacations and all of her free time so I could realize my goal. How lucky I am to have two mothers.

Special thanks to my brother, Bruce, for making me laugh as he did when we were kids, even through the rough times of the writing of this book.

I would like to thank those persons who allowed me to enter into their world and took this journey with me to make this book possible so others may also heal.

I would like to thank my first therapist, Harvey B. Bezahler, M.D., whose continued guidance, patience, and forcefulness with issues concerning my father, *even when I resisted*, helped to shape the first pages of this book. He has been and will always be an instrumental force and a guiding light in my professional and personal success.

I acknowledge several of my mentors and colleagues, without whose contributions this book would never have been written. My effectiveness with patients is a mixture of their ideas and mine.

Special thanks to Dr. Florence Lieberman, my professor in 1975, who taught me everything I know about children, then inspired me to follow in her footsteps by teaching and publishing my theory, "Family Play Therapy." She has always been a role model and inspiration to me.

I'd like to thank Dr. Gerda Schulman for her belief in me.

How can I find the words to thank Thomas F. Fogarty, M.D., family therapist, mentor, and friend, who both professionally and personally changed my life by watching me and helping me mature as a family therapist? He taught me family therapy not only with patients but with my very own family. His astuteness, expertise and nonjudgmental manner helped not only my parents and myself, but my brother as well.

What can I say to Philip J. Guerin, M.D., Director of the Center for Family Learning, for helping me to learn about the necessary role of the "family of origin" in healing? Without his wisdom, this book surely would never have been written nor our legacy ever uncovered. In my second year of family-therapy training, when I proudly said to him, smiling, "Dr. Guerin, I've done *all* the work on my family of origin" (beyond what was required), he answered, "You've only just begun." And how right he was. He started the wheels turning for the work to which I have now dedicated my life.

Special tribute goes to the memory of Murray Bowen, M.D. His great contributions to the field, especially the use of the genogram and the three-generational model that I have followed, led me to the subject of this book.

Thanks to Selma Petker, M.S.W., and Judith Gilbert Kautto, C.S.W., of the Center for Family Learning, for their warmth and their helpfulness.

Special thanks to Susan Burden, C.S.W., family therapist, with whom I continued my family-of-origin work and who saw me through some very rude awakenings.

Very special recognition to Lori Gordon, M.S.W., founder of the PAIRS Foundation (Practical Application of Intimate Relationship Skills) of Falls Church, Virginia, under whom I studied, and to her husband, Morris Gordon for their invaluable communication tools, variations of which appear in this book.

Special gratitude to Dr. Harville Hendrix for allowing me the honor to study IMAGO Relationship Therapy, so that I could share it with my patients and contribute to his dream of IMAGO becoming a household word. Many of the exercises in this book have been adapted from Dr. Hendrix's work, as well.

Special thanks to Bruce Wood, for his friendship and for taking the time to teach me IMAGO Relationship Therapy, and for introducing me to Dr. Hendrix. Thanks, too, to his lovely wife, Pam Wood, for enlightening me, and for her friendship.

And to Sheila Gutter, Director of the Stress Management and Wellness Program for the United Federation of Teachers, who helped me reduce my stress during the writing of this book—such a dear friend who was there when the going got rough.

And to Hillary Eth, past president of Step Families of America, for standing behind me and helping me reach the goals that we strived for together; from the seminars and workshops I gave to Step Families of America evolved some of the insights in this book.

Special acknowledgment to Hy Steirman, who supported me when I lost sight of the difference between the donut and hole.

To Gloria Michels, for her faith in me and continued support, which always bolstered me when I became discouraged.

To Jinny Schreckinger Rushnell, for her patience, time, and support in helping me through some tough deadlines.

To Tony DeLorenzo, private investigator specializing in adultery, and to his assistant, Dawn Ricci, for their help.

Special thanks to John J. Vallone, for all his help and generosity in meeting deadlines—and in dealing with emergencies that occurred on the weekends in the Poconos.

I'd like to thank everyone who took the time to fill out my survey: "Adultery: The Forgivable Sin." I would also like to thank Leah Adler, rebirther, for her contribution and her continued interest in my topic. I would like to thank Siegfried Wiedemann, who accepted Federal Express packages and helped with emergency deadlines; Norman and Gail Goldman, for their true caring and support during the difficult writing times of this book; Jita and Raymond Jablons, for being good sports and testing out the skills in this book; Dennis C. Watkins, for his help and wonderful attitude; and Stanley Kaplan, of the Stanley Kaplan Courses, for his excellent advice when I really needed it.

To Lory Lazarus, Mark McColl, Sanam Hoon, Karl Stewart, Mara Yuk Casey Yu, and Nancy Jones of the Institute for Relationship Therapy, who always took the time to answer questions and be of assistance, thanks for supporting me in this project.

And special thanks to those who inspired me: My sisters-in-law, Jean Weil and Jean Eaker; my brother-in-law, Kenny Weil; Barbara Bevando Sobal, Esq.; Jacalyn F. Barnett, Esq.; Ray Scheck, M.S.W. for his interest and helpful additions; Arlene Klapper, C.S.W.; Ronnie Schwartz for her insights and encouragement; Kaluska Poventud, producer of "Good Day New York"; Andrew Scher, producer, for his contributions and the many hours he spent with me.

And special thanks to Kim and Joel Schechter, for their

friendship, creative ideas, and brainstorming, all of which added to the book's richness; to the memory of Gail Neuberger, for her interest, smiles, and pep talks; and thanks to my secretary, Lisa Caccavale-Soto, for the homestretch typing done in the wee hours of the morning to meet surprise deadlines.

Thanks to Dan Levy, my first editor.

Thanks to Gail Kinn, my editor, who stuck by me through tough times. Her incredible patience, talent, and guidance made this project possible. Special thanks to Eileen Schlesinger, my new editor who inherited this book, for her patience, understanding, and dedication.

I would like to thank my publisher, Steven Schragis, for the opportunity to write and publish this book; and Norman Kurz of Lowenstein Associates, for his time, effort, and help, which I greatly appreciate.

Special tribute to the memory of my beloved maternal grandparents, Sarah and David Brodkin, who are ever in my thoughts.

Special tribute to my paternal grandmother, Pearl Eaker, for her courage and perseverance, which I emulate; and to the memory of my paternal grandfather, for his warmth.

Special thanks to the Brodkin, Bernstein, and Eaker families.

THANKS TO LYNN LANGWAY, MY FAVORITE WORDSMITH WHO HELPED ME IRON OUT THE WRINKLES IN THE MANUSCRIPT. HER DEDICATION, LOYALTY, TALENT, AND SUPERHUMAN EFFORT MADE WHAT YOU ARE READING POSSIBLE.

And finally, deepest personal thanks to Oprah Winfrey and her staff, for allowing me to share the teachings of this book—forgiveness—on several of her shows.

The names of persons and places have been changed to protect identities.

Introduction

This book is for everyone who has suffered the agony of betrayal or who fears she or he will. It is for singles, couples who are married and couples who are not; almost one half of my practice is composed of unmarried couples whose relationships have been ruined by infidelity or its shadow. It is for the deceivers as well as the deceived; for the lovers as well as the beloved.

One night when I was seven years old, I was shocked awake by a strange and terrible sound: my mother and father were screaming at each other in the living room. The subject of the argument, I now know, was his persistent infidelity.

My mother, who usually played the role of family peace-keeper, had finally found a clue so blatant that not even she could ignore it—that classic brand of the adulterer, a scarlet smear on his shirt. She knew it was lipstick; absurdly, he kept insisting that it was only a smudge of dye from the red pistachio nuts that were served at his late-night poker game.

"It's pistachio nuts!" he insisted. "You're lying!" she snapped back.

I couldn't bear to hear anymore, so I clapped my hands over my ears and burrowed under the covers. And there I stayed, emotionally, for the next twenty years. I never allowed that awful memory to surface—not in five years of psychotherapy, not in marriage or divorce. I fled so far emotionally from the whole scene that I never even discussed my father with my therapist. Yet I also *overcorrected* wildly, marrying a man who was not very interested in sex with me, let alone with other women.

But then, when I was twenty-seven, two things happened to tear those bedcovers away. First, my mother walked out on my father, refusing to return until he agreed to stop having affairs and start counseling, Later, while I was putting together a family history for a graduate course I was taking in family therapy, I brought my parents along, and *I made the dramatic discovery that my parents had also buried their own unbearable memories.*

Under the skillful questioning of my mentor, the family therapist Thomas Fogarty, M.D., my mother broke down and confided that she knew her father had carried on an affair with the family's housekeeper.

Then, as Dr. Fogarty prodded him gently to recall his childhood traumas, my father, too, began to cry. Haltingly, as Dr. Fogarty urged him to confront the emotional emptiness inside himself, my dad finally voiced the shameful secret he had carried alone for more than forty years.

"I came home unexpectedly at the age of ten and I saw this strange man with my mother. By the looks on their faces and their strange behavior, I thought my mother had been unfaithful to my father," my dad revealed.

At that moment, I began to see that adultery—much like alcoholism or abuse—is a multigenerational plague.

My father, too, had tried to hide under the covers. But even without acknowledging his terrible secret—not in eight years of therapy—he was driven by it, trying to get back at his mother and avenge his father by sabotaging all his other relationships with women.

My mother, meanwhile, had tried to remake her own childhood through marriage, picking a playboy who resembled her father and then struggling to reform him.

I, too, was scarred by my burdensome secret; while I had not committed adultery, I could not trust men and was terrified of intimacy.

Since those personal revelations, I've seen my insights confirmed again and again in twenty years of practice as a family therapist. I've counseled more than a thousand couples. The vast majority (80 percent) came to me because one partner or the other had been unfaithful.

In nine out of ten cases, my patients and I determined, over the course of therapy—sometimes involving four generations, grandparents as well as parents and children—that at least one partner was the adult child of an adulterer—an adulterous mother or father.

Very few patients recognized this family connection when they started. Most of them knew, but didn't want to know, just like me. And like me, almost all of them had concealed their knowledge—and the emptiness and pain it engendered—deep inside themselves, even during therapy. Then one day, they or their loved one had an affair—and began to confront their secrets, with the help and support of other family members.

Traditionally, adultery destroys any relationship it touches; 65 percent of adulterous marriages end in divorce.

But it doesn't have to be that way. **Only 2 percent of the couples I counsel divorce after they discover that adultery has been committed.**

Why? Because I don't agree with the anguished accusation made by many a wounded spouse: "You've committed the unforgivable sin!" *My patients, parents, and I have demonstrated the opposite. Adultery can be a very forgivable sin.*

I don't condone it, under any circumstances—how could I, when I've seen how far its damage can spread? But I do believe it is often the result of an inherited behavior pattern, not a free choice; the adulterer is trying desperately to fill emotional needs that went unmet by his own parents.

An affair is a symptom of an unresolved problem that can be passed on from generation to generation. In an amazingly high proportion of cases, that childhood wound was inflicted by parental adultery; in others, by the early death of a parent, divorce, or other event that left the grown-up child feeling abandoned or betrayed.

Remember:

PEOPLE WHO ARE NOT IN SOME KIND OF PAIN DO NOT COMMIT ADULTERY.

Hoping to ease the ache of his or her emotional emptiness, the adulterer reaches out to new partners just as others reach for food, alcohol, or drugs. I dedicate this book to them and to you.

If you are the adulterer, you must reconnect to those who have hurt you, those whom you have hurt, in order to become credible again and learn to defeat your dangerous legacy.

If you are the betrayed, you must reunite with those who have hurt you—including your parents—and stand up for yourself to build a deeper, more satisfying love.

I wrote this book because I believe adultery is always a mistake, but also understandable.

We must put aside our Puritan need for punishment, the stocks, and the Scarlet Letter. Adultery threatens us on a deeper level than punishment can heal. *For all of us, infidelity raises the terrifying specter of abandonment, a threat so basic to our sense of stability since childhood that we dare not look it in the face.*

One of my major goals is to help eliminate the fear, the

shame, and the blame surrounding adultery; only then can we deal with the real reasons it happens and lessen the terrible trauma it inflicts.

With enough love, hard work, understanding, and commitment, adulterous patterns can be broken. We can find healthy ways to deal with our emotional pain. We can learn to fight fairly, to forgive, and to achieve a greater intimacy. We can reconnect to our partners as well as to the parents who—usually unknowingly—injured our psyches during childhood. Both our relationships and our children can not only be saved, but strengthened.

My parents, retired now, have reached real love and are happier than they've ever been; I am closer to them; and twenty years after my divorce I am remarried to a wonderful man who has helped me overcome my fears. My brother, too, has happily remarried after twenty years.

Our experiences with family therapy changed our lives. Without all of us working together, my secret, my father's secret, and my mother's secret could have been buried forever, and our destructive legacy passed down to yet another generation.

Now I want to help *you* to leave the darkness of betrayal behind and step into the light.

To this end, I offer you both my personal experience and my professional knowledge of what works.

Reader Alert

- If your spouse or sweetheart has been cheating, or displays a wandering eye...
- If you yourself have been tempted to stray, or find yourself thinking too much about another...
- If you know, or suspect, that you have a family heritage of illicit love...
- If you find yourself involved, again and again, with lovers you cannot fully have...

- If you cannot commit to a faithful, loving relationship or any relationship…
  this book is for you.

Our Goals

In the first part of the book, we'll explore the real motives behind adultery, when and why it happens and to whom, and what preventative actions can be taken.

In the second part, I'll show you how to survive and even grow from this shattering experience, with patient-tested exercises to help you fight, communicate, heal.

You can conquer this devastating problem and prevent it from happening again to your children or your children's children. You can unlock your family secrets and resolve your hidden conflicts.

THE UNFORGIVABLE SIN CAN BE FORGIVEN.

Let me show you how.

Danger Signals

As you've just seen, my own mother was tipped off to her husband's affair by a classic clue: the smudge of lipstick on the collar.

There are other obvious tip-offs: hang-up calls and whispered conversations; strange charges on the phone bill or credit card; the uncharacteristic whiff of alcohol or an unfamiliar perfume; diminished interest in sex.

Sometimes, though, the evidence can be more subtle—and apply to the adulterous individual of either sex.

Quiz: Danger Signals to Watch For

1. Is your spouse or partner spending a lot more time away from home—on business trips, at meetings, nights out with the boys or girls? Are lunch hours very leisurely?
2. Is he or she going to work earlier and coming home later? When you call, does the office have trouble tracking your mate down?
3. Do sales conferences or evening classes seem to last longer than they used to?
4. When at home, is your mate restless? Does he/she suddenly spend an extraordinary amount of time doing "good deeds," as if to make up for guilt?
5. When you are together, do you find yourself talking less and watching television more?

Tattle Tales
6. Does the name of a particular colleague or neighbor suddenly start cropping up regularly?
7. Alternatively, does someone who used to rate numerous mentions barely get mentioned at all?
8. Does your loved one fill you in on all the insightful or clever comments made over lunch by a friend of the opposite sex,
9. Or start coming up with uncredited opinions and jokes that don't sound like his or her own?

Cosmetic Clues
10. Has your loved one suddenly discovered a boundless desire to work out at the gym? Or a new dedication to a diet?
11. Has he/she changed an accustomed way of dressing, wearing spiffier ties or sexier lingerie?

12. Has your partner suddenly tried a makeover previously resisted—getting contacts, wearing short skirts, letting tresses or nails grow long?
13. Has he gotten a hairpiece or implants? Has she streaked her hair?

Bed Alert
14. Do you make love more or less often than usual?
15. Are new techniques suddenly appearing or being asked for?
16. Has foreplay changed? The afterglow?
17. Has your lover stopped using sexual endearments or pet names?

Storm Watch
18. Has your loved one become very secretive about credit-card slips? Does he race to debrief the answering machine—in private—and head you off to answer the phone?
19. Is your partner provoking more fights, or being more belligerent when you argue?
20. Has the level of fault-finding risen?
21. Do your children show signs of stress: clinging, nightmares, or hyperactivity?

If you answered yes to more than three of these questions, your relationship is heading for choppy waters...and may be on the rocks.

Adultery: The Forgivable Sin

· 1 ·

What's the Problem?

Adultery can strike a relationship with the force of a heart attack. Like the victims of cardiac arrest, when you discover that your partner has been unfaithful, you are staggered by the agony you feel. Your ability to trust, your self-esteem, and your very will to live may be destroyed.

Just like heart disease, adultery is both shockingly common and on the rise—especially among women. **According to most recent surveys, between 50 and 70 percent of American men and 30 to 50 percent of American women will be unfaithful at some point; one partner will have an affair in approximately 80 percent of all marriages.**

Among committed, unmarried couples, the incidence of infidelity is higher still. Even if you're not married, you are committing adultery when you betray the love and trust you have promised to your partner.

But heart attacks are not always fatal—and neither is adultery. Cardiac patients can survive and even thrive, once they find a healthier way of living. You can do the same by finding a healthier way of loving.

I know how wrenching adultery can be, because I watched it nearly tear apart my own family.

I also know from my own experience, both personal and professional, that adultery can be a forgivable sin.

My dapper father and beautiful mother married for love, but they were nearly undone by their hidden family legacies of infidelity. Over and over again, my father cheated on my mother; over and over again, she took him back—until, one day, she'd had enough.

Although neither knew it, both were playing out destructive scripts written during their own childhoods. Repressing his boyhood suspicions that his mother had been involved with another man, my dad nonetheless avenged his father by becoming a philanderer himself. Distrusting all women, he became a fugitive from intimacy.

My mother, whose father had trysted with the family maid, became an avid pursuer of her husband, repeatedly forgiving his transgressions.

I, too, was damaged. Once, when I was just a little girl, I overheard my parents arguing bitterly about adultery. I promptly buried the memory, but was haunted by it for the next twenty years. I married a man I thought would never cheat on me, because he expressed so little libido; after divorcing him, I remained terrified of commitment.

None of us revealed these secrets, though, until we came together at the Center for Family Learning in New Rochelle, N.Y., where I was getting my advanced certificate in family therapy.

Our experiences with family therapy changed our lives as, one by one, we confronted the painful emptiness childhood had left within each of us.

Since then, my mother and father have rekindled their love and grown closer to each other, as well as to their own parents and to their two children, my brother and myself. Never before had I experienced such satisfying relationships with every member of my family—and I have finally been able to build a loving, intimate marriage with Jeff, my second husband.

Opening my own heart and mind to the problem has

taught me this much: **Fidelity is not a guarantee that love persists, nor is infidelity a sign that love has faded or died. In fact, adultery can even be a way—albeit dysfunctional— to try and stabilize a floundering relationship.**

Without all of us working together, our destructive inheritance might have been passed along to yet another generation.

Now I hope that you, too, can benefit from what we have learned. For twenty years, I have been helping my patients recover from the heartaches of adultery. These methods work: *Ninety-eight percent of the couples I treat remain together after the discovery that one (or both) partners have had an affair, as compared to only 35 percent of the general population.* My patients are in the majority.

Adultery is flooding society today as never before. The subject is inescapable, aired in movies and on television, in pop songs and commercials. Yes, Calvin Klein touts his fragrance, "Eternity," but he's also selling "Escape" and "Obsession" with his sensuous models. ("How perfect and foreign he was," intones one "Obsession" commercial, quoting D. H. Lawrence. "This was the glistening forbidden apple...")

The supermarket tabloids are no longer the only outlets for sex scandals; in recent years, the so-called respectable press has also dished out the dirt on everyone from princes (Charles and Diana, Andrew and Fergie) to politicians (President Bill Clinton and his alleged alliance with Gennifer, George Bush and his alleged alliance with Jennifer) to movie stars (Woody Allen and Mia Farrow).

Our appetite for gossip about extramarital escapades reveals our profound ambivalence. On the one hand, we claim to honor the Seventh Commandment; on the other, adultery is rampant in the entire population. More than twenty states still classify adultery as illegal, and often it's even used as a murder defense.

We continue to cluck publicly about the topic—the revelation of Gary Hart's amorous adventures with Donna Rice, for example, derailed his run for the presidency in 1988. And in a recent poll by *Psychology Today*, 92 percent of those sampled declared monogamy to be "important" or "very important."

Forty-five percent of those same people, however, also admitted they had had an affair!

Some of our contradictory attitudes are downright dangerous. It might seem logical to believe that the spread of AIDS has scared us all into toeing the line. In my experience, though, that is—unfortunately—not the case. In fact, just the opposite is true. I hear of more and more adulterous affairs in which the married partner is seduced by the single woman.

In a twisted form of logic, many seek out married lovers because they convince themselves that they are less likely to be infected by husbands than by bachelors, who may have logged more partners in recent years.

Overall, women are starting to catch up with men in the rate of infidelity. In 1980, for instance, a poll of *Cosmopolitan* readers indicated that 50 percent had had at least one affair; in 1987, sex researcher Shere Hite found that 70 percent of women married for more than five years had been unfaithful.

Now that the overwhelming majority of American women work outside the home, there are more opportunities to meet other men, and more temptations at business lunches, sales conferences, late-night projects, and the like.

Do Girls Just Wanna Have Fun?

What most concerns me about this trend is the current argument that you can't be a liberated woman unless you fool around. Several books have celebrated the supposed "guilt-free" affair as a way for women to find and nourish their thwarted sexual selves.

But haven't we heard all this before, from Erica Jong among others?

Nobody hates the double standard more than I do—why should men who cheat be lionized as dashing rogues, while women are slandered as sluts?

But who wants to be an equal in emptiness? The women quoted in these books are supposedly looking for the kind of no-strings sexual pleasure that men have enjoyed in the past. Well, first of all, I don't believe that exists for men, either—as we'll soon discuss. Second, *if you read the women's words carefully, you notice that they repeatedly cite their search for someone to talk to.*

It's not just sexual satisfaction they're seeking—it's intimacy and validation. And that's what we should be able to find, or demand, at home.

You don't often stumble upon this sort of emotional satisfaction in a casual affair—and the women who do find it there usually want to make the arrangement permanent. Women who are unfaithful, I notice, are more likely than men to be using an affair as a cry for help—an escape hatch from an unhappy marriage or having never married for love.

Ironically, this new push for women to be more casual about sex coincides with a new desire among men for more caring and closeness. Now that the mass of baby-boomers are hitting their forties, our society is becoming more middle aged on average—and in mid-life, studies consistently show, women generally want more independence, while men want more intimacy.

Maybe instead of trying to compete in some kind of sexual sweepstakes, we should be striving for a rapprochement.

Fearful Attraction

Why is adultery so frightening and yet so fascinating? In part, because we recognize the appeal of it. We grew up in triangles, competing for our mother's attentions with our fathers and our siblings, and vice versa. That taught us, deep inside, to be terrified of abandonment and to resent sharing. **We never quite give up on the childish fantasy that somehow, someday, we'll find someone all our own who only wants us. This is the destructive fantasy that keeps us looking for love in all the wrong places.**

Despite our familiarity with adultery, we still don't understand it very well. It's time we stopped alternatively ignoring, excusing, and condemning this epidemic. To deal with a problem, you've got to comprehend it first.

Let's start by correcting some dangerous misconceptions that have taken root in the conventional wisdom.

THE FIVE BIG FALSEHOODS ABOUT INFIDELITY

1. Adultery is about sex.

You'd never cast Deena as a femme fatale: plump, fortyish, and cheerful, she radiates motherly warmth, not body heat. That, however, was just her allure for Fritz, a 50-year-old lawyer, who'd been having an affair with his paralegal for several years.

In therapy with his pretty wife, Sheila, Fritz confided that he missed the affectionate love his mother had given him, which had compensated for the coldness of his demanding, philandering dad. (Not so coincidentally, Sheila's own aloofness reminded him of his father.)

I cite their case as evidence for an underrated fact.

ADULTERY DOES NOT NECESSARILY SWEEP LOVERS ALONG ON A FLOODTIDE OF PASSION.

In most couples, the wandering spouse is trying to stave off an empty feeling left by childhood hurts and frustrations—especially if he/she is the adult child of an adulterer, like Fritz.

Frequently, the sex is better at home and the marriage partner is at least as good-looking. **When I conducted a random survey of a hundred Americans, for example, only one of those who admitted to having affairs gave "poor sexual relationship" as the reason. More often, the attraction was emotional rather than physical.**

In a growing number of cases, especially in the workplace, there's no sex involved at all—although I'd classify these consuming office friendships as affairs. The definition of adultery in *Webster's Third International Dictionary* is "voluntary sexual intercourse between a married man and someone other than his wife, or between a married woman and someone other than her husband," the second one is "unchastity of thought or act." However, neither of these seems quite right and I find the *Webster's* second definition of infidelity closer to the truth. It includes "a breach of trust...unfaithfulness to a charge or a moral obligation" as well as extramarital sex.

To my mind, that means ANY breach of trust (not necessarily between married people).

Intercourse doesn't have to take place. In fact, these "affairs of the heart" can be even more treacherous than the purely physical kind. **Women, particularly, are inclined to leave their husbands when they feel a strong emotional bond with another man.** This is especially likely if they did not marry for love or if they want to get out of a marriage but don't know how.

Any activity or relationship that drains too much time and energy from life with your partner is a form of unfaithfulness. That may include workaholism, obsession with children, sports or gambling addiction, as well as emotional liaisons.

2. Adultery is about character.

We used to look down on alcoholics as being weak characters who just couldn't say "no." Now it's widely accepted that alcoholism is an addiction, a disease that's often hereditary, and not a moral failing.

I'm not saying that a penchant for adultery can be passed

along genetically in the same way—but **there is mounting evidence, noted in my practice as well as that of others, that there is an emotional dynamic in adulterous behavior that is transferred to the children.**

Youngsters can sense that something is wrong even at a very tender age—children as young as two years old have stunned their parents by babbling about Mommy or Daddy leaving. They may base these intuitions on seen behavior or over-heard words, as I did. Years later, these adult children of adulterers will act out their legacy without even knowing it, through their own or their partners philandering or other dysfunctional behavior.

Carl Learned Too Young

Consider the case of Carl, a minister, who left his wife, Marsha, for her best friend. The situation was particularly agonizing for this couple, who considered fidelity to be essential to happiness and morality. Both had grown up with adulterous parents—she knew it, he did not at first—and both were playing out the unfinished scripts of their troubled childhoods.

Marsha's father humiliated her mother repeatedly, flaunt-ing his mistresses, one after another. He also belittled his daughter, criticizing her weight, her hair, her makeup, until she felt inadequate as a female. "You're too skinny, no one would ever want you," he'd sneer. "Your nose is too big—you'll never get a man."

When she learned of her husband's alienation, she could only conclude that her father had been right—and she withdrew further into her silent hurt.

Carl, meanwhile, remained unconsciously furious at his mother for having had an affair. He had been glad to find a woman like Marsha who cared as much as he did about being true to each other. But inside, he still wanted to punish women for what his mother had done—and he was unknowingly compelled to do so by repeating her sins.

Those who commit adultery are not adulterated human beings, any more than alcoholics are degraded by their excess. They want not to be judged or punished by society. They punish their families and themselves enough. Rather we should destigmatize this behavior and deal with the forces that motivate it.

3. Adultery is therapeutic.

Surprisingly often, adultery may be a misguided attempt to keep a troubled relationship going. The emphasis, however, is on *misguided*.

YOU CANNOT FIX WHAT'S WRONG WITH A RELATIONSHIP BY ADDING ANOTHER COMPLICATION.

Graham, for instance, said he was happy being married to Helen, who was a splendid mother to their four children—although no longer interested in sex. He had an affair with a colleague at his civil service job and tried to pass it off as therapeutic: *"I feel that getting the sex I need elsewhere will keep me happier and more satisfied and will save our marriage."* Helen, it turned out, didn't share that view—which is why this couple showed up in my office.

There's an alarming tendency among some therapists to suggest that infidelity can stabilize a marriage. Some adulterers, meanwhile, contend that extracurricular sex will teach participants how to be better lovers, to everyone's joy.

That's a theory fondly embraced by those who seek a rationale for their wanderings, of course. **But the notion that infidelity can enrich a relationship would be laughable if it were not so destructive**. It's a lot like the man who kept bashing himself on the head with a hammer because it felt so good when he stopped.

Yes, you may work your way through an affair to find after it's over your marriage is stronger—but it requires incredible honesty and dedication, and it's painful.

Insisting that going out and sleeping around in order to

find fulfillment in your marriage is a pathetic self-delusion. It doesn't work; that's why adultery results in divorce 65 percent of the time.

Survivors of adulterous affairs know the price that has to be paid. I know of no case where the survivors of a marriage tested in this way would consider doing it over again—unless you count Henry and Celeste. They divorced because of infidelity and married their paramours. Then they ran into each other at a charity ball—and began an affair. The communication was better and so was the sex. They remarried and—when last seen—were faithful and happy this time around.

Even their reunion will not last, however, unless they can handle the inner needs that drove them apart in the first place. **Those who do not understand why they stray will never find it easy to stay (with anyone).**

4. Adultery is harmless.

We have so many cute nicknames for the subject. Among the most printable: playing, fooling, or sleeping around, hanky-panky, swinging, flings, one night stands, sowing your wild oats, getting a little on the side.

These euphemisms help perpetuate the most dangerous myth of the guilt-free adultery movement: that no one is hurt by it, that it's just a simple pleasure.

Some argue that it's almost recreational, like sports. Dan, for example, rationalized: "I'm not hurting my wife because she doesn't know about it and the relationship means nothing. It gives me a lift, it gives me excitement. It's like a thriller—like going to the movies."

Don't pass the popcorn, please.

Yes, extracurricular sex is a pleasure—one of the reasons betrayers have such a hard time giving up their lovers is that it feels good and it's flattering to have someone around who always puts you first, someone you don't have to nurse through the flu or argue with about the mortgage. **Forbidden sex can seem to be nothing more than a delicious indulgence, like chocolate cake.**

In truth, this "simple pleasure" is more comparable to cocaine than chocolate—addictive and potentially lethal. Everyone in a family suffers from an affair—particularly the children.

Once discovered, adultery hits a whole family like a massive hurricane, smashing homes, shattering trust and self-esteem, battering the young.

I listen to the agonizing fallout every day:

- ▶ "I don't ever want him to touch me again."
- ▶ "I'll tell the kids what a whore their mother is."
- ▶ "I have nothing to live for."

There may be illegitimate pregnancies, traumatic abortions, diseases like herpes to contend with. Many patients feel suicidal:

- ▶ "I've given everything I had to Jack and the kids and now here I am, forty-two-years-old and finished," wept Eileen, who barely survived an overdose of sleeping pills when she learned about her husband's affair.

You can compare the compulsion to have affairs to addictions to alcohol, drugs, or the excessive need to work all the time. As with all addicts, the denial is very great.

Even if your spouse or partner does not know you are cheating, he/she will be hurt. Those who say, "Hey, it's relaxing, it's fun, and as long as I'm not emotionally involved, what's the harm?" are sadly mistaken. *They are depriving their partners of energy and intimacy. They are escaping from the need to grow and change within their relationship. They are being dishonest and will erode their emotional bonds.* If you really value the people you profess to love, you do not want to betray them and make fools of them.

We can understand the reasons for having affairs without excusing them. The damage that they do can take generations to undo; *infidelity masks the real problems in the individual and the relationship.*

It's time we stopped rationalizing that affairs make us feel good, that we just can't get all our needs met in one

person. It's time we stopped propagating the notion that women will feel more fulfilled through extramarital sex. What about the legacy to the next generation, and to *their* children?

We must recognize that the epidemic of adultery poses as serious a problem to emotional health as incest or child abuse. And indeed, today, it can threaten our very lives.

If you think adultery is innocent as long as the victim isn't informed, witness the case of my patients Veronica and Kyle.

They were about to marry after living together for three years. Just before the wedding, though, Veronica was feeling extremely tired, and she went for a checkup.

Her blood tests revealed that she had a full-blown case of AIDS.

Her fiancé was found to be HIV-positive, although symptomless; a secret bisexual, he had contracted the virus from a man he'd picked up in a bar.

5. Adultery has to end in divorce.

Even if you never forget, you can learn to forgive. Ninety-eight percent of my patients are able to renew their marriages, after they dedicate themselves to the exercises and develop the attitudes you'll read about in Part 2 of this book.

If you can come to recognize the real motivations for adultery and learn the skills to deal with the underlying problems, you will get through this trauma.

That's what happened to Carl and Marsha, once they got beyond their politeness and their ingrained uncommunicativeness. She had to learn to face yesterday's hurts and today's anger; he had to resolve his need for revenge.

Their road back was bumpy: he moved in with his mistress and refused to go to counseling for a year, while Marsha rebuilt her life and confidence. Eventually, however, he saw how much he still loved his wife—and was able to convince her of that fact.

He even signed a special fidelity contract which we drew up

together, stating that he understood that if he ever strayed again it would be the end of their marriage.

Jolted by their experience, Carl and Marsha's marriage was nonetheless renewed—and when last I saw them, they were expecting their first child.

• 2 •

Why Do Fools Fall in Lust?

W hen you take your marriage vows, you swear to love and honor each other until death do you part. Today, about half the brides and grooms who make that vow break it. Why?

That's something I always try to find out when couples first meet me for a therapy consultation. I always ask the following questions:

- **How** did both of you get to this point with each other?
- **Why** weren't you getting what you needed from each other instead of going outside the relationship for some kind of validation?
- **How and why** were you not there for each other?
- **Why** did one of you find it necessary to get attention by having sex with someone else, thus creating a crisis?

EXCUSES, EXCUSES

In answering the above questions people have given me just about every possible rationale and excuse under the sun.

16

Some are so predictable, they could come right out of a soap opera. To those who offer them, though, they doubtless seem like fresh insights.

- ▶ My wife/husband doesn't understand me.
- ▶ She nags me.
- ▶ She's too involved with the kids.
- ▶ He works all the time.
- ▶ He always puts his mother first.
- ▶ She's a good woman, but she's not interested in sex.

Sometimes I hear romantic fantasies about the affair.

- ▶ It's the fairy-tale world I couldn't find in marriage...it's never-never land.
- ▶ It's a perpetual vacation.
- ▶ It's a sedative, a tranquilizer.
- ▶ It's as exciting as a roller coaster.
- ▶ I feel so exhilarated, so alive.

I've also heard some real lulus. The topper, I guess, was the man who straightfacedly insisted in front of his wife that the only reason he'd carried on with a woman during a business trip is that he was trying to be polite. When the stranger asked him whether he wanted to join the mile-high club, he declared that he thought she was talking about frequent-flyer miles. So he said sure—and then, of course, he couldn't back out. (For the many nonmembers among you, the mile-high club is composed of those contortionists who have managed to make love in the rest room or seats of an airborne plane.)

The Blame Game

Many philanderers want to blame their behavior on society and today's climate of sexual permissiveness. "Everyone is doing it!" protested Mark, a salesman, who'd had several affairs with customers. While his wife, Alice, sobbed in my office, Mark went on: *"My wife is not realistic. It's impossible to be monogamous in today's world. I don't know any women that I meet during the day who aren't cheating on their husbands. They are all ready and willing to hop into bed."*

He never seemed to realize that there was something desperately wrong if that was indeed the case—not only with Mark and Alice, but with all these women who craved the admiration and approval of strangers.

For the record:

There do seem to be some enduring differences in motivations between the sexes. According to a 1992 study of adulterous men and women by Baltimore psychologist Shirley Glass, **75 percent of the men said that sexual excitement was a justifiable reason to stray, as compared to 53 percent of the women. Women who excused an affair as "falling in love" were likewise in the majority: 77 percent, as against 43 percent of the men.**

Many who wander like to pin their problems on a partner's changing ways—or, conversely, on their failure to adapt. Frequently, for instance, successful businessmen decide to dump their original spouses and marry younger women once they hit the top; *Fortune* magazine calls these mid-life replacements "trophy wives."

Bill and Jeanette had something of the opposite situation. For years she was a bland and passive partner, moving when Bill's computer job required it, wearing what he wanted her to wear. But then, with her kids almost grown, the women's movement influenced her—and she began to bloom. She finished college, then got her M.B.A. Hired by a blue-chip brokerage firm, she became a top manager. She made a six-figure salary and spent plenty on herself, buying designer suits and the obligatory BMW.

Bill, meanwhile, was just treading water, and her success didn't make him cheer. Instead, he had an overt affair with one of his colleagues to try and regain his power. Jeanette refused to go back to her meek old ways: instead, she insisted that they consult me.

It is normal to feel, after living with someone for a long time, that he/she or the situation has changed. **Getting rid of a person doesn't get rid of a problem.**

Why not readjust the meaningful relationship in which you've already invested so much time and love? Why not amend your original contract? Talk with your spouse, re-negotiate—as Bill and Jeanette finally did.

Infidelity often happens when one person seems to be controlling the other and breaking the clauses of the original marriage pact. The betrayer wants to regain clout and—maybe unconsciously—be discovered, so he can make his feelings known.

That's what Larry was trying to do to get the attention of his aloof wife, Wendy. When he chastised her about her extravagance, she spent what she wanted anyway—and often lied about it. After years of seething inside, Larry had an affair in an attempt to make her sit up and take notice. She did, but not quite the way he had in mind—she contacted a divorce lawyer.

THE REAL REASONS WE STRAY

The common motives for infidelity are as varied as the lovers themselves: boredom, loneliness, frustration. Some-times, an affair is prompted by revenge. Fran's husband, Bennett, was carrying on with the wife of a good friend. Fran decided to pay him back in kind. "Why should I leave and have to support the kids? He makes half a million dollars a year. I'll just find myself a little amusement."

People are often driven to affairs at an important transi-tion in their lives—a birth, a death, a decade birthday.

On the seventh anniversary of Leon's marriage to Alicia, his parents broke the news that they were breaking up their thirty-two-year union. Feeling abandoned and deceived,

Leon diverted his hostility to his wife. Just as a child may act naughty to punish a parent, he had an affair with one of Alicia's girlfriends in order to get even with his mother, who had precipitated the divorce.

Season's Cheatings

Sometimes, a simple opportunity may seem to be the culprit. Time and again I have seen a rise in affairs during the Christmas/Chanukah/New Year's holidays, when there are so many cocktail parties strung with mistletoe. High expectations for fun combined with the stress of job and family run high, and inhibitions are correspondingly low. Partygoers may be just as tempted to indulge in extramarital sex as they are to pig out on fattening food.

On the surface, that was the case with Tara, who had an interlude with the president of her company after the Christmas party.

Beyond the obvious motivation of too much champagne, something else was driving Tara. It turned out that Christmas made her blue. She was nostalgic for the close, warm holidays of her childhood. Now she and her husband, Van, lived far away from her family, and he was too busy to take time for a visit. He was also too preoccupied with work to listen when she tried to explain her despondency. *Her fling was an attempt to win her husband's notice and, failing that, she sought intimacy with someone else.*

Like Tara's escapade or Leon's involvement, most infidelity is tied to our childhood yearnings. **We may be looking to reclaim a lost utopia, a time of love without responsibility. Or—in the majority of affairs—we are trying to compensate for the hurts, frustrations, and unmet needs of our youth.**

Nine times out of ten, that hurt and hunger were inflicted by some form of abandonment and oftentimes by an adul-

terous parent. Most of the time, however, we do not know—
or readily acknowledge—this fact.

**IT IS THE HIDDEN MOTIVE THAT DRIVES SO MANY PEOPLE
INTO UNFAMILIAR ARMS.**

Take two patients who came to me claiming they had been
struck by love like a bolt from the blue.

Simone, a fashion executive, had been married for seven
years when she fell for a client. "I couldn't stop the feeling. I
knew it was wrong, but I just couldn't help it," she said.

Hal tumbled for a vice president at his bank. "We have so
much in common. She understands me and everything I am
trying to do. I tried to stop myself, but I couldn't," he
declared.

**What neither smitten lover realized—until I brought
their parents in on our therapy sessions—was that they
were carrying out their family legacies of illicit love.**

Both were the adult children of adulterers.

STATES OF THE AFFAIR

Whatever their obvious or hidden motives, affairs tend to
fall into one of the following categories.

THE PSEUDO-INTIMACY AFFAIR

Almost all of us have problems developing and sustaining
intimacy. This affair is the most common type of entanglement. That's especially true for men, who are supposed to
separate from their mothers and declare their independence
in order to identify with their fathers. This abrupt schism
creates an intimacy problem with women their entire lives.

These fugitives from intimacy often create a triangle to use as a wedge to drive between themselves and their partners.

Sam, for example, bounced back and forth for years between his wife, Sandra, and his mistress, Lillian.

The only child of a doting mother, he thought he wanted his wife to hover over him just as his mother had done. After too much cosseting, however, he felt suffocated—just as he sometimes had as a boy. Then he'd flee to Lillian—who, ironically enough, looked like a younger version of Sandra— until she also started demanding too much attention and sex, at which point he would return to Sandra to search for his mother.

Five times he left home; five times he came back.

"I know I am not acting right," Sam told me. "I feel like I'm going crazy."

What Sam couldn't find in either Sandra or Lillian was really himself. It was the emptiness inside that he was trying to fill. Only when he and his wife confronted the hidden motives could they reconcile.

Single men are even more likely to run from commit- ment—as many a single woman can testify.

Ryan, for instance, broke up with his girlfriend of four years, Ginny, when she brought up the dread topic of marriage. He moved in with Heidi—but then proceeded to cheat on her with his old flame.

He was doing just what his philandering father had done to his mother. He didn't want to, but he had internalized the lesson that intimacy means loss, betrayal, and hurt.

THE PEACEKEEPING AFFAIR

A large percentage of affairs are desperate dysfunctional efforts to keep a relationship going. **"If I can find what I don't get from my mate elsewhere,"** the adulterous party reasons, **"I won't have to break up my happy home."** As we've seen—and will again—this simply doesn't work for long.

Many of the peacekeepers are couples who sidestep conflict at any cost. No matter what happens, they delude themselves into thinking that a polite marriage is a happy one.

When his wife, Winnie, told him she was involved with another man, for example, T.J. said in astonishment, "But we never fight. I thought she had everything she ever wanted...She never told me she was unhappy."

That's precisely the point at which I tell them it's time to start talking no matter how loudly. **Infidelity often hits hardest at marriages that are the most tranquil on the surface**...the kind where voices are never raised in hostility. If you don't know your mate's needs, disappointments, and fears, he/she may turn to an affair as a cry for help. Although woman are more likely than men to reason in this way.

Often, one partner goes along with seeming docility for years, storing up resentments. Unfaithfulness may be an effort to provoke a fight—maybe the first and much-needed fight of the marriage.

Maria and Neil had one of those mannerly marriages. She was deeply unhappy that he ignored her and the children, but was unable to tell him so. Instead, she gained nearly a hundred pounds. He, meanwhile, couldn't bring himself to tell her how neglected he felt, and how repulsed he was by the weight she had gained. Instead, he protested by sleeping with someone else.

Remember, where there is no fighting, there is no passion. And if you are not very close to your spouse, there is room for someone else.

THE ESCAPE HATCH AFFAIR

Many women find themselves unable to leave a loveless or even abusive marriage. An affair can force the issue and help them out the door.

That was what happened with Jan. Married to a man she did not love, who had been handpicked by her controlling mother, Jan was miserable but frozen in place. She had a blatant affair with her daughter's orthodontist; she had sex with him in his chair, and made sure to go out of her way to be gossiped about by his dental assistant. Subconsciously she knew that once her husband and mother found out, they would hasten to end the marriage.

This is one of the few motivations for adultery that frequently ends in divorce—just what the refugee so desperately wants.

IF SOME ADULTERERS WANT TO WALK OUT THE DOOR, OTHERS WANT TO LEAVE THE CLOSET.

With the welcome increase in openness about homosexuality, I see more and more gay people unwilling to continue a heterosexual charade. They may use an affair as a way to declare themselves.

Some spouses feel less threatened by a same-sex lover, believing these are needs they could never satisfy. But some feel mortified, taking the affair as a personal affront to their own sexuality.

That's how Jim felt when Ashley left him for Brittany, whom she'd met in a writing workshop. He said he could compete with another man but not with a woman—he simply felt repulsed.

However, latent homosexual drives are not always recognized by the adulterous party.

Judd slept with Serena, the wife of his best friend, Albin. The two men had been buddies since high school. When Serena told Judd that sex with Albin was waning, Judd offered her his services. When I asked him why, he replied, "I did it out of love for Albin and Serena," with no guilt or awareness of deeper meanings. After that, fantasies of having a sexual relationship with Albin surfaced.

THE LOVE-SEEKING AFFAIR

As we've seen, those who do not marry for love and then find it elsewhere are especially likely to leave. Not surprisingly, they either can't or won't dedicate themselves to saving their marriages.

Another large contingent of adulterers, however, *think* they're looking for love—or at least sexual excitement— when they're actually trying to feel better about themselves.

A lot of these affairs happen when end-of-decade birthdays roll along—the thirtieth or fortieth for women, the thirtieth, fortieth, or fiftieth for men. Suddenly, the "celebrants" find themselves feeling especially empty, wondering, "is that all there is?"

Aging men will frequently look for sexual reaffirmation, like Harry. A virgin when he married, Harry felt over the hill on his sixtieth birthday, and took up with a younger woman to see what he might have missed.

At age forty-five, Norman decided he wasn't going to miss anyone—or anything. A hotel owner who'd been married fourteen years, he started coming on to guests five years later when he turned fifty. "Sex with Lois had become boring," he said. "Now I appreciate her more. I've learned new techniques, and it's exciting to have sex with a new woman."

Married sex doesn't have to be boring, of course. To keep it interesting, you've got to be willing to invest time and effort in your relationships, just as you do in your children, careers, and tennis games.

Many women who hit a bumpy milestone, on the other hand, look for emotional solace. Younger people of either sex, having less unsatisfied curiosity about the subject, are also likely to want emotional involvement when they stray.

Barbara badly needed to boost her self-esteem when she turned thirty. Stalled in her career as an executive secretary, she was often left alone by her workaholic husband, Jeff. That simply amplified her girlhood insecurity, brought on by parents who'd always favored her beautiful and smarter sister (and a father who'd had a long-standing extramarital liaison). She wanted desperately to have a baby, but couldn't get pregnant despite repeated infertility treatment.

She sought refuge in an affair with her Casanova of a boss, Jerry, and kept covering up with flimsy pretexts about working late every night. Finally, as she almost wished would happen, Jeff came down to her advertising agency, convinced the security guard to let him in—and discovered Barbara and Jerry cavorting on a couch.

In a way, I think she was relieved. Jeff finally began to cut back his workload and spent time trying to salvage their love. They succeeded—once they went back to the formative experiences that had made them act that way.

THE COMPULSION-DRIVEN AFFAIR

Sometimes, a Don Juan or vamp is just ducking intimacy— but in a small proportion of cases, these are genuine sex addicts, using promiscuity as a fix to numb their pain. This category of adulterous behavior remains controversial, but there is some intriguing research on the subject. Dr. Jennifer Schneider, a Tucson physician who specializes in the treatment of addiction, reported at the Southeastern Conference on Alcohol and Drug Abuse in 1991 that the cases of sex addiction she has seen fit the classic definition of addiction: compulsive behavior with a loss of ability to stop, despite adverse consequences such as a loss of a relationship or job. "The person is obsessed with the pursuit and conquest of the sex object and devotes a great deal of time to it," she reported. About 80 percent of the self-reported addicts are men, but she believes women with this disorder are reluctant to admit it.

Whatever its cause, a compulsion toward unrestrained sexual intercourse is not only abnormal but dangerous both to the betrayer and the betrayed because of, among other things, the possibility of infection with AIDS and other Sexually Transmitted Diseases (STDs).

THE AFFAIR CAUSED BY PHYSICAL OR PSYCHOLOGICAL PROBLEMS

In many cases, medical conditions, substance abuse, or psychic disorders, such as depression or manic depression, may spur partners to affairs or general promiscuity.

Burt, for example, went through two divorces—and was about to have a third—before I stepped in and sent him off for diagnosis, suspecting manic depression. Once Burt was properly diagnosed and medicated, his wife, Laura, realized that her husband's promiscuity, compulsive spending, and mood swings were neither deliberate nor her fault, and she was able to join wholeheartedly in family therapy.

When last I saw this couple, they and their two little boys were doing well.

HOW TO FIGHT FAIR

Good manners often interfere with good relationships. You should never let politeness stop you from letting your mate know how you feel.

But don't simply let fly with your fury—that can be destructive, too.

You'll learn more about channeling the anger that arises from adultery in chapter 9 (page 108).

Here, though, are some rules of combat, based on the work of Dr. Harville Hendrix and Lori Gordon, M.S.W. of PAIRS.

1. *Ask permission.* "I'd like to have a talk with you. Is this a good time?" Then say what you want to discuss.

2. *If the present is not the right time, reschedule within twenty-four hours.* Make an appointment—"Let's talk about your mother's visit tomorrow at 6:00 P.M."

3. *Make it time-limited.* We all have different thresholds of emotional as well as physical pain. Either participant can call a time out if the pressure gets too great.

4. *No ignoring allowed, because if one person thinks there is a problem, there is a problem.* Partners must acknowledge each other's comments and look each other in the eye. No television or other distractions allowed.

5. *Defuse the situation by dealing with "I" sentences rather than "You" sentences.* The second almost always lead to blame, and shut down communication. People hear better when they're not being attacked!
EXAMPLE: **Do say:** "I feel very insecure when you flirt with other women at parties." **Do *not* say:** "You lecher—you always make a fool out of yourself at every party we go to!" You want to keep the communication as safe as possible.

6. *Listen to and echo what your partner says in order to lessen miscommunication.* Prove you're hearing it by repeating what's being said after every few lines: "So what you're saying is you felt neglected and had an affair?" If you don't understand, keep asking questions and repeating until you do.

7. *Validate the other person's feelings.* This doesn't mean you always have to agree, just that you recognize that your partner really does feel the way he does, and that it rings true and is logical from his point of view.
EXAMPLE: **Do say:** "I understand you turned to an affair because you missed me and I was always working."

8. *Empathize—feel what your partner feels, put yourself in your partner's place.*
EXAMPLE: **Do say:** "I can see how abandoned you must have felt."

9. *Never punish the person for opening up by belittling them or criticizing in any way—or they'll shut right back down again.* (Don't throw it back at them later, either.)

EXAMPLE: **If she says:** "I think you are having an affair," **He should *not* say:** "That's the stupidest thing I've ever heard!"

10. *Take responsibility for making your wants and goals clear.* Be as honest as you can without being hurtful—think about how this will sound to the other. *Be as positive as possible; your message will be received more favorably.*

EXAMPLE: **Do say:** "It was important to me when you took care of your weight." **Do *not* say:** "You're so fat you disgust me!"

Thank the person for the gift of sharing and caring enough to confide. Then hug them when it's all over.

All in the Family

This above all, to thine own self be true.
—William Shakespeare

W hatever the ostensible motive, adultery is almost always a family affair. **I see scores of troubled couples every year, and in nine out of ten cases, either the straying partner, his/her mate, or both partners had adulterous parents. Most often, my patients are unaware of this fact until we uncover it in therapy.**

A bent for infidelity is not transmitted genetically, like blue eyes or high blood pressure. It is an emotional inheritance, passed along in subtle ways. Many adulterers can't or won't make the family connection immediately. Like my father and myself, they repress their suspicions or dark memories until multigenerational therapy brings the family secret to light.

Sometimes the suggestion that a predilection for adultery is passed along through family behavior patterns is greeted with skepticism or embarrassed laughter. "My grandfather? My mother? Fool around? That's crazy!" an uncomfortable client will scoff. "Bring them into therapy? They'll never come. It's ridiculous. It won't change anything."

But think, for a moment, about a few of the famous cases you already know about. Take the Kennedys: the swashbuckling patriarch, Joseph Kennedy, boasted openly about his long liaison with actress Gloria Swanson, and tales of the amorous adventures of his sons John, Bobby, and Teddy abound.

After years of randy bachelorhood, John Kennedy finally married Jacqueline Bouvier, whose own dashing father, "Black Jack" Bouvier, was a notorious ladykiller. Neither marriage nor the presidency seemed to cramp John Kennedy's lecherous style—he reportedly frolicked with Marilyn Monroe, Angie Dickinson, Judith Exner, and other glamorous girlfriends, sometimes right in the White House.

Nowadays, there are ample indications that these disturbed patterns of intimacy have been passed down to Old Joe's grandchildren. The young Kennedys have had more than their share of divorces, arrests, alcoholism, and drug abuse— although it must be noted that Jackie Kennedy Onassis seems to have raised her own two children, Caroline and John, Jr., in a way that minimized their sad legacy.

Royal Suites

Consider England's royal family, where mistresses—or "confidantes," as they're discreetly called—have long been accepted and even acclaimed. Look at the result: pain.

If, as reported, Prince Charles has been cozying up to his favorite confidante, Camilla Parker-Bowles, instead of spending time with Princess Diana, they are just following family tradition. After all, when she first met the prince, Camilla exclaimed, "My great-grandmother was the mistress of your great-grandfather! I feel we have something in common."

History bears her out. Great-grandma was Alice Keppel, the inamorata of King Edward VII. Keppel was so favored in royal circles that the queen even summoned her to say goodbye to the dying king. (She saucily described the etiquette of her role: "A royal mistress should curtsy first, then leap into bed.")

Charles has a royal flush of relatives with a roving eye (see genogram, page 43). His uncle Edward VIII (also known as David) dallied with assorted married ladies until he fixed on one, Mrs. Wallis Simpson of Baltimore. She divorced, he abdicated for "the woman I love," and they spent the rest of their lives as the exiled Duke and Duchess of Windsor.

Then, of course, there are the varied romantic scandals involving his aunt, Princess Margaret, his sister, Princess Anne, and his princely brothers, Andrew (supposedly cuckolded by his duchess wife, the notorious Sarah Ferguson) and Edward, whose prolonged bachelorhood keeps provoking rumors—and palace denials—that he's gay.

Princess Diana has her own long legacy of illicit love. Five branches of her family, the Spencers, are descended from the illegitimate offspring of King Charles II. More immediately, her mother, Frances, left home to marry her lover, Peter Shand Kydd, when Diana was only six years old. Her late father, Earl Spencer, later remarried Raine, the daughter of romance novelist Barbara Cartland, but Diana never felt close to her stepmother.

If the princess also found consolations outside her marriage, as rumored, then she, too, was following a well-worn family path.

Denying the Truth

With the possible exception of a few jaded aristocrats, no one can believe the possibility that a mother or father would ever break their marriage vows. **Initially, many adulterous patients deny that there is any infidelity in their family background. Then, they tell me their families won't cooperate—and even if they will, that won't change anything.**

The truth emerges only after they have talked with their parents, as well as their partner, in an honest, loving fashion. The truth often cuts deeply, but also sets them free—free to forgive their elders and themselves.

Over and over again, I've seen these confrontations work their magic, reconciling estranged families and ending decades of pain.

This is what happened to Harvey, his wife, Sabrina, and their whole family—*but only after I used a childhood memory of my own to help unlock their stunning secrets.*

A Mother's Tears

Harvey, a fifty-year-old economist, was having an affair with his assistant, Terri. His wife, Sabrina, a teacher, learned about the arrangement in a most unsettling way: Harvey had taken his teenage son out to dinner with his paramour, and the boy couldn't stop raving about Dad's gorgeous friend.

That meeting precipitated the crisis that brought them to my office. I asked them both if their parents had ever been unfaithful.

"I believe my father ran around," Sabrina volunteered, while Harvey looked on in surprise.

"There was no adultery in MY family!" Harvey interjected loudly "No way!"

He did allow, though, that his mother seemed to cry a lot—every day, in fact. When I asked him why, he said vaguely, "Well, it was the Depression, and I guess she was worried about money."

I wasn't satisfied with that response, and the mention of the unexplained tears nagged at me.

Then I remembered how my maternal grandmother used to weep whenever one of the characters on the soap operas we watched together strayed into an affair. Her tears were heartfelt and out of all proportion to the melodrama on the screen. I later learned that both her father and her husband had inflicted great hurt with their extramarital romances. At the age of ten, I resolved right then and there that I wanted to grow up and become a therapist, to try and keep affairs from making people cry.

That memory gave me a clue to what might be wrong here, and I urged Harvey to bring his eighty-year-old parents in for a joint session. His mother, Mina, soon revealed why she was always crying: "My husband was having an affair with his secretary. I wanted him to fire her, and he insisted she was too valuable to the company to let go."

It was the same ultimatum that Sabrina had given Harvey thirty years later!

Harvey just sat there with his mouth agape, stunned. "I didn't know," he whispered. "I had no idea until this minute."

But if Harvey had no conscious memory of this difficult period in his parents' marriage, he was nevertheless affected by his mother's chronic distrust of his father and the tension it generated. In adulthood, he was unconsciously trying to work out what he had not coped with as a youngster.

This revelation turned out to be helpful to everyone involved. Harvey and Sabrina resolved to rebuild their marriage. Harvey realized how distant he had felt from his father, Herbert (and later, from his own wife). In one very moving session, he hugged his father for the first time, said "I love you, Dad," and told him how he'd longed to do that all his life.

Herbert cried, but still felt too inhibited to return the embrace. Then I told him that, by doing so, he could break down the walls that were ruining Harvey's marriage. Suddenly, he threw his arms around his middle aged son, and shakily said the magic words, "I love you."

His father's declaration allowed Harvey to give up the solace his lover provided, to leave her, and to revive his relationship with Sabrina.

Eventually, Herbert and Mina revived their own marriage, too—demonstrating that it's never too late to forgive. She revealed how the incident still plagued her sleep. "I have been crying every day for the last thirty years," she told him, noting that she could never forget the way he had laughed off her fears. He was aghast to realize that she was still haunted by it. He apologized, she began to trust him, and they began to renew their relationship.

It can be difficult to make the family connection even if you're a professional therapist. I certainly suppressed it, through many years of analysis, and so did my patient Jane.

A Therapist Hides the Truth (from Herself)

Jane is a successful psychologist, although not a successful lover. Unmarried at age thirty-five, she consulted me to explore why she could not sustain a relationship. She was constantly pursuing married men—and as soon as they acted seriously interested, she'd drive them away.

In therapy, she admitted that she both adored and hated her doctor dad. Eventually, she recalled how he had carried on with his nurses and patients. Her mother had remained aloof, trying to ignore his promiscuity. Jane's breakthrough came when she finally realized that she was trying to punish him—and her mother—by seducing other husbands. Her father joined her in therapy, and they began at last to move toward a healthy relationship.

Only then was she able to pick men who were available.

TEACH YOUR CHILDREN WELL

But how do children find out about affairs if parents are reasonably discreet?

They have very sensitive emotional antennae that can tune in bad vibrations in one of two ways. **Even if they don't witness a traumatic scene—a shouting match, a stolen** embrace—children are very likely to sense that their parents are tense, remote, preoccupied, and focused on someone else.

With guilt, secrecy, lust, and other powerful emotions churning through him, the deceiver no longer has time to turn full attention to the children—and they pick up on that. (Although the alternative—busying yourself with the little ones to assuage your guilt and avoid your spouse—can also be a warning signal.)

While parents try to shelter children from upsetting situations, youngsters are usually aware of family difficulties at some level. Sheltering can cause mistrust. *Remember, children pick up nonverbal cues—even if they don't let on.*

This can happen at a very tender age. I was consulted by the worried parents of two-year-old twins, Sam and Steven, who had suddenly turned defiant—throwing tantrums, smearing excrement on walls. Their mother was involved with another man, but neither parent could believe that the twins had any idea.

"How could a two-year-old know?" the father asked. "Let's all play and we shall see," I said.

Sure enough, the secret came out during Family Play Therapy. I asked Sam to place dolls and furniture in a dollhouse. The child placed one male figure on the sofa, and a female figure on the bed. Then he placed another male doll beside her, and began hitting it, yelling "No, no" and "Mommy bad." His brother, Steven, threw the extra doll on the floor and stepped on it and broke it.

I said, "Yes, you are mad at the man who is Mommy's friend."

At that point, the distressed mother admitted that the twins had met "Mommy's friend"—and evidently had picked up on the fact that he was a threat to their security.

The outcome: through Family Play Therapy and seeing things through the eyes of the children, the couple was able to recognize and deal with their marital problems. **In many** cases, the child is the patient, but the parents need the help.

Clarissa, the Family Symptom-Bearer

That was certainly the situation with three-year-old Clarissa. She was brought in by her parents showing symptoms of emotional distress: nightmares, bed-wetting, separation anxiety. Whenever her mother, Eileen, tried to leave the room, the little girl would cling to her leg and scream.

We soon discovered that what she was really afraid of was losing her parents, who were drifting toward separation. She was aware of increasing coldness and hostility around her, and she was fearful that her mother was going to walk out the door and disappear for several days, just as her father, Brad, repeatedly did.

Both Brad and Eileen were adult children of adulterers, although each was unaware of the fact. Brad had acted much like his father, indulging in numerous romances. At the time the family came in, he had a new entanglement with someone he'd met at a seminar.

In therapy terms, Clarissa was her family's "symptom bearer." Her behavior focused attention on a destructive family secret, which the entire family has to grapple with if this dysfunctional cycle is to end.

Sibling Revelry

There are other influential family ties besides the parental one that may be destructive to future marital satisfaction. Recent research indicates that our relationships with siblings can also exert a powerful force on relationship patterns.

Infidelities can reverberate through a family, as it did with brothers Paul and Len: when one started an affair, the other followed suit later that month.

Reverberation is especially strong, of course, if the siblings are twins, like Seth and Sydney. Seth was married four times, and cheated on every wife—much to Sydney's disgust.

She was determined not to repeat her twin's unfaithfulness. Still, seeing that much treachery in someone she loved made her afraid to get too close to any man.

So she picked someone who would be "safe": a handsome airline pilot named Aldo who was married with five children. He couldn't abandon her because he was never hers in the first place.

The illicit legacy had been handed down—sideways, from Seth to Syd.

Passing on the Guilt

The adult child of an adulterer never quite outgrows the fear of abandonment, the shame and guilt they feel for being somehow responsible. If a child cannot erase those fears, he/she may spend a whole lifetime repeating a parent's mistake.

The legacy of unhappiness in love will continue unless and until these problems are faced—and faced down. That is by no means an excuse for adultery—but it is a reason to try to understand and to forgive.

TRACE YOUR OWN FAMILY TREE

How can you tell where adultery runs in your family? Take a family history and use a **genogram** to chart it. (I recently ran into comedian Mel Brooks who, in his inimitable way, referred to this as a "Cheat-o-gram.")

A genogram, a tool developed by Murray Bowen, M.D., and named by Philip Guerin, Jr., M.D., is a diagram of your family's relationship patterns.

By providing a structural framework, the genogram offers a nonthreatening way for family members to open up. No, they might not tell all at the Thanksgiving dinner table. But everyone likes to talk about the old days. You may be surprised at their frankness when you sit down one-on-one or in small groups. Make copies of the following blank genogram to chart each partner's family history.

One Family's Genogram

This is what happened with the L. family. Their grandmother was referred to me because she was extremely depressed and threatening suicide. At first, she was so withdrawn that she would not even look me in the eye. Once we started filling in the genogram, though, the information began to flow.

She blurted out a secret she had never told any of her children—**her firstborn daughter had been born out of wedlock.** She had been having an affair with the man she later married, who was supposed to wed another at the time. "That was the start of all my problems," she said.

Gradually, we widened the therapy circle, including her children and grandchildren. There were plenty of tears as we traced the transmission of adultery, alcohol, and cocaine abuse, and how her descendants had acted out a legacy they knew nothing about. All her children were having affairs, and her grandchildren were troubled by bed-wetting, hyperactivity, and suicidal feelings.

Still, the sessions also encouraged much warmth and laughter—and in the end, this matriarch declared, "I was so ashamed. I kept the secret for fifty years. Now I feel so light."

I suggest that you embark on such a project yourself. Start by telling family members why you are seeking the information. "My husband and I have hit a rough patch in our marriage. I became involved with another man as a way to

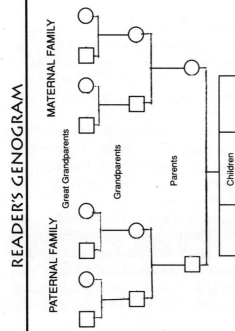

READER'S GENOGRAM

PATERNAL FAMILY   MATERNAL FAMILY

Great Grandparents

Grandparents

Parents

Children

	Men
□ ○	Women
A	Adultery
A+	Adultery while wife is pregnant
NA	No adultery
P	Promiscuous
R?	Rumors of outside romantic interests
D	Emotionally distant relationship
---	Lover
—	Parent-child relationship

/	Marriage
//	Separation
‖	Divorce
♥	Remarriage
＊	Happily married
＊＊	Clone of adulterer in the family
⊘ ⊠	Simultaneous separations and divorces within family
	Death of parent (form of betrayal/abandonment which
	alters intimacy)

NOTE: PATTERNS OF ADULTERY AND SEPARATION/DIVORCE GO HAND-IN-HAND

ask for help. But we don't want to break up, and I'm hoping you will help us search for patterns in our past that will help us and heal us."

What to Record

▶ Start with yourself and your siblings. Who were you all named for? What were your nicknames? Did you have an identity: a title within the family, like "our little social worker"? (That was mine.) Then work backward, through your parents and aunts and uncles to your grandparents.

▶ Record ages and dates of pregnancies, births, deaths, severe illnesses, marriages.

▶ Record separations, divorces, affairs, and other traumas, such as miscarriage or job loss.

▶ Ask about the character of family relationships:

Who was particularly close to whom—your mother to her little sister, your brother to a generous uncle?

Who was distant? Who was "frozen out" by the rest of the family—not on speaking terms? Why?

Does your family have a pattern of holding grudges?

Were there family feuds? Over what?

Did the family have any "black sheep"? Who were they and what were their problems?

Were there triangles within the family—Dad always sided more with your brother, but you were Mom's pride and joy? Aunt Hettie vied with your mom for your little sister's affections?

Are there physical resemblances among generations? Other similarities? Who "takes after" whom?

Do you see your parents in your spouse? Do they? What about your parents' relationship compared to your own. Do they echo each other?

Do you get the sense there are family secrets?
What do you suspect they are?
▶ Enter the information, in abbreviated fashion, on
a chart like the blank genogram (page 40). You
will be surprised at how repetitive patterns leap
out. In my case, for example, I noticed that every
one of my mother's siblings was divorced, as was
my father's brother; my two maternal aunts had
split with cheating husbands during pregnancy.
**Adultery and divorce go hand in hand as you
will see in Princess Di's and Prince Charles's
genogram, my genogram, and probably your
own.**

CHARLES AND DIANA'S "CHEAT-O-GRAM"

The odds for marital bliss were heavily stacked against
Charles and Diana. Adultery and sexual scandal run rampant
through both their families. And although divorce was once
unheard of for royal family members—it's why Edward VIII
abdicated, after all, and why Princess Margaret couldn't
marry her true love, divorced Group Captain Peter Townsend, back in 1955. But times have certainly changed. Every
royal marriage since that of Queen Elizabeth II herself, forty-
five years ago, has ended in, or been reported on the brink of,
divorce.

Consider this troubled couple's most immediate ancestors:
King George V married **Queen Mary** and had six children, including:
Edward VIII, who romanced several married women, then
married twice-divorced **Wallis Simpson**. After his abdica-
tion, the throne passed to:
King George VI, who married **Lady Elizabeth Bowes-
Lyon**. There were no rumors of infidelity in this popular
couple who had two daughters.

ROYAL FAMILY GENOGRAM (CHEAT-O-GRAM)

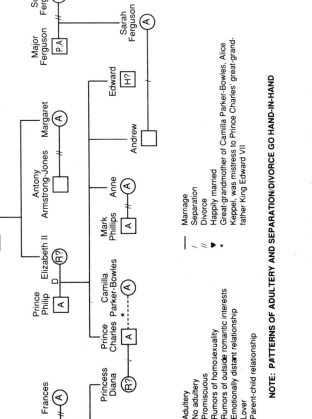

A   Adultery
NA   No adultery
P   Promiscuous
H?   Rumors of homosexuality
R?   Rumors of outside romantic interests
D   Emotionally distant relationship
- - -   Lover
| Parent-child relationship

| Marriage
//   Separation
➤   Divorce
*   Happily married

Great-grandmother of Camilla Parker-Bowles, Alice Keppel, was mistress to Prince Charles' great-grandfather King Edward VII

NOTE: PATTERNS OF ADULTERY AND SEPARATION/DIVORCE GO HAND-IN-HAND

Margaret, who married photographer **Antony Armstrong-Jones** after an affair with Captain Townsend ended. She was linked to several men during their marriage, including would-be singer Roddy Llewellyn. The couple divorced in 1978, after having two children, **Sarah** and **Viscount Linley**.

Elizabeth II, who married **Prince Philip of Greece**. Rumors about her handsome consort, born of aristocratic but impoverished stock, have hummed for years, since he began traveling by himself in 1956. One supposed inamorata was actress Merle Oberon, who entertained the prince without the queen at her Mexican villa in 1968. No juicy photos or backstairs confirmation that he fools around has ever surfaced in the press; however, there has even been some printed speculation that the queen has sought more than racing advice from her racing manager, Lord Porchester, in days past. No incriminating evidence here, either.

What IS known is that, like many blue-blooded couples, Elizabeth and Philip maintain separate bedrooms and live virtually separate lives. They have four children (from youngest to eldest).

Prince Edward—unmarried; he has been battling rumors of his homosexuality since 1987, when he quit the Royal Marines. He has not been publicly linked with any women, and he is often accompanied by male friends from the world of theater in which he works.

Prince Andrew, Duke of York. Joshed by all the tabloids as "Randy Andy" after his escapades with former porn starlet Koo Stark, Andrew married **Sarah Ferguson** in 1982.

Unlike her sister-in-law, Diana, who had supposedly been certified as virginal at the time of her marriage, Fergie had a certifiable past; she'd lived for years with Paddy McNally, a writer and race car driver, and traveled with the international jet set. Her family background also included some fast company.

Fergie's parents, **Major Ronald** and **Susie Ferguson**, split after Susie became enamored of Hector Barrantes, a widowed Argentinian polo player. The major remarried, but was pilloried in the press as a regular client of a posh London "massage parlor." He then had an affair with Leslie Player, who verified this in a book she later published.

In 1992 the duke and duchess separated, following the publication of photos of Fergie vacationing with American tycoon Steve Wyatt while Andy was off doing naval duty. Those snapshots were innocent-looking, but not so subsequent published pictures of a topless duchess lolling about with her American "financial advisor," John Bryan, in the south of France. (He was shown sucking on her toe.) That summer, Andrew and Fergie moved into separate abodes. They have two daughters, **Beatrice** and **Eugenie**.

Princess Anne married horseman **Mark Phillips**. They had two children, but were constantly dogged by scandal. The British press reported her having an affair with her police escort, Peter Cross, which led to his dismissal in 1981.

In 1989, Phillips was linked to House of Commons call girl Pamella Bordes; in 1990, to a stable girl. He was also accused of fathering an illegitimate child in New Zealand (and of an affair in Canada).

Anne, meanwhile, had a fairly open friendship with royal equerry **Timothy Laurence**, whom she married after her 1992 divorce from Phillips.

Prince Charles, the Prince of Wales. Millions watched Charles marry **Diana Spencer** in a splendid 1981 ceremony. Widely pronounced a fairy-tale, the marriage does not appear headed for a happy ending.

Charles, who was linked to many beautiful women before his marriage, has reportedly continued his liaison with Camilla Parker-Bowles, whom he met in 1972. (She is married to Army Brig. Andrew Parker-Bowles.)

Diana, the mother of princes **Harry** and **William** (Wills), did not seem to take the royal tradition of adultery in stride. She has reason to fear extramarital entanglements and possible abandonment.

Diana's mother, **Frances**, left home when Diana was only

six, to marry Peter Shand Kydd. His wife sued for divorce, citing Frances as co-respondent. Her late father, **Earl Spencer, Viscount Althorp**, won custody of Diana and her three siblings (including sister **Jane**, who dated a supposedly smitten Charles before Diana did) after a ferocious court battle.

Her father later remarried **Raine**, the daughter of romance novelist Barbara Cartland, but Diana's relationship to her stepmother was icy.

Her brother, **"Champagne Charlie,"** also had a notorious affair after his much publicized wedding to a top model.

Diana has reportedly had warm relationships with various male friends who were assigned to teach her to ride or to be her bodyguard. The most titillating friendship, however, was with chum James Gilbey, a British businessman; newspapers printed transcripts of what was allegedly a taped phone call between the two. He called her Squidgy and drooled a lot of romantic nonsense; she expressed great affection for him. (The tapes, picked up by a ham operator from Gilbey's car phone signal, were never authenticated.)

At the time we went to press, the prince and princess were legally separated, and many are betting on an eventual divorce.

MY FAMILY GENOGRAM

I will show you that infidelity is very common, not some singular shame that has happened only to you. **Families are like mobiles, and when one part is touched by a trauma, such as adultery or divorce, the whole system reverberates in response.** As you will see on my genogram, after I got divorced, my parents got separated, and my brother divorced. When my paternal uncle got separated, his daughter followed suit.

GENOGRAM OF AUTHOR'S FAMILY (AUTHOR'S CHEAT-O-GRAM)

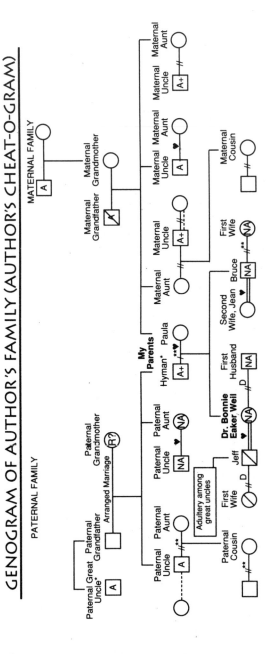

A   Adultery
A+   Adultery while wife is pregnant
NA   No adultery
P   Promiscuous
R?   Rumors of outside romantic interests
D   Emotionally distant relationship
---   Lover
| Parent-child relationship

—   Marriage
/   Separation
//   Divorce
‖   Remarriage after 20 years
♥   Happily married
*   Hyman, clone of favorite uncle
**   Simultaneous separations and divorces within family
⊘   Death of parent (form of betrayal/abandonment which alters intimacy)

NOTE: PATTERNS OF ADULTERY AND SEPARATION/DIVORCE GO HAND-IN-HAND

When I first met my husband, Jeff, he said there was no infidelity in his family. It was only after we were preparing this genogram six years later that we discovered there were two relatives on his side who had divorced after having affairs. You, too, will doubtless discover many surprising similarities you share with your partner and family.

Not all adult children of adulterers follow suit—neither my brother, Bruce, nor I did. But both of us developed problems with intimacy, and both of us divorced our first partners and waited twenty years to remarry!

Note that divorce was pervasive all around my parents. My father's brother, and my mother's sisters and brother, all divorced. Both my maternal aunts divorced their husbands after discovering that they had cheated on them while they were pregnant; my father also cheated while my mother was pregnant with Bruce.

My parents somehow stuck it out, however—and through family therapy, we were all able to come together again, stronger than before.

We refused to carry the damage of our legacy. You can arrest yours, too, once you understand your family patterns and how they have contributed to your pain.

• 4 •

The Secret Script

One day when Jarrett was fifteen, he was sent home from school with a feverish case of the flu.

As he entered his house, he heard dance music playing on the radio. He followed the sound into the living room, where he saw an unbelievable sight: *his mother dancing cheek to cheek with a stranger, her eyes closed in ecstasy as he caressed her breasts.*

The oblivious twosome didn't hear Jarrett come in, and he backed out silently and retreated to his bedroom.

There he lay frozen for hours, agonizing over whether to tell his dad. He didn't want to hurt his father, but he couldn't bear to keep him in the dark. And he didn't want to alienate his mother—but he couldn't condone her betrayal. When his father finally arrived, he blurted out the story. His mother was furious, his father ashen.

After that day, however, the family never discussed the incident again. Within a week, it was seemingly forgotten—and deep-sixed by Jarrett.

Fifteen years later, he decided to marry Claudia, a dark and pretty woman who greatly resembled his mom. He then proceeded to deceive her by taking a lover.

When the couple sought my counseling, Jarrett cried, saying he couldn't choose between the two women he loved.

Why was he so conflicted?

After many sessions, that teenage memory suddenly flashed back to him. Eventually, with his mother cooperating at sessions, he learned to forgive her and himself, and renewed his marriage. **Until he could reconnect with that first woman in his life, he could not sustain closeness or keep faith with any other female.**

Adult Children of Adulterers

Like Jarrett, many adulterous partners are playing out a secret script, reenacting scenes they may not even recall.

Although they do not always know or admit it, they are often the adult children of adulterers.

When they grow up, these children usually react to parental philandering in one of two ways: they **repeat**, or **retreat**.

The repeaters have affairs themselves, hoping to rewrite their script or avenge the cuckolded parent—as Jarrett did.

The retreaters shrink from intimacy, refusing to get hurt by another loved one ever again—as I did.

These patterns are not inevitable, though; those who recognize these impulses can resist them. Once the secret is out, the legacy loses its power.

This is what I tell the many adult children of adulterers who come to me before they marry or move in with someone they love. "Am I going to be able to spend the rest of my life with this woman?" one son of an unfaithful mother asked me. "Or will I keep looking for someone new?" Not, I reassured him, if he and his sweetheart are willing to work together. *Those who discuss fidelity before marriage, studies suggest, are most likely to achieve it.*

Every child reacts somewhat differently to the disclosure

that a parent was untrue. But these are some recurring scenarios for each type of relationship between an adult child and an adulterous elder. You may not fit directly into one pattern, but be a combination of one or several of the following.

ADULT DAUGHTERS OF ADULTEROUS FATHERS

When they reach maturity, the daughters of unfaithful fathers often feel—among other things—angry and mistrustful of all men. Frequently their self-esteem is damaged and they respond in predictable ways.

They may try to re-create their fathers by marrying an adulterer—as my mother, her two sisters, and her mother all did—**or they may imitate him by becoming faithless themselves.** Still others may repudiate him by picking someone whom they think will NEVER EVER stray. That is what I did with my first husband—a strategy referred to in family therapy terms as an *overcorrection.* Or they choose unavailable men or become the lover in a triangle. If the daughter is overly close to the father and the parents have a distant marriage, the fantasy to take dad away is acted out by stealing other women's husbands.

Shelly's Story

My patient Shelly, a fifty-year-old accountant, sought to boost her self-esteem by reforming her husband (and revising her childhood script). Her father, a hardware merchant, slept with many of his customers and frequently slapped her and her mother around.

It may seem astounding that Shelly—who above all people should have known better—would marry Tom, a TV producer who cheated and abused her. But like the children of alcoholics who marry alcoholics themselves, Shelly was hoping to make the story turn out differently this time.

Instead, the tale threatened to spin into yet another generation. Her twenty-five-year-old daughter, Lucy, had just become engaged to Mark, a young man with similar traits. Mark was, however, at least willing to become involved in family therapy with his fiancé, her parents, and his. Perhaps by coming to terms with his own abusive legacy (his father had broken his nose when he was a boy), he can alter it.

ADULT DAUGHTERS OF ADULTEROUS MOTHERS

These women often fear close relationships and are attracted to adulterous, distant, or married men. Some become predatory and promiscuous, trying to get back at or identify with their mothers by taking away other women's husbands; some retreat into frigidity.

Karen's Story

Karen tried both approaches. As a young girl, she was humiliated by the snickers about her hot-to-trot mother that echoed around the country club.

She vowed to be different and was until after college, when she started sleeping around. Then, shamed by gossip herself, she made an overcorrection and stayed celibate for two years. She finally started therapy when she met a man she wanted to marry, but found herself turned off by sex.

ADULT STEPDAUGHTER OF AN ADULTEROUS STEPFATHER

The charges and the countercharges in the case of Woody Allen, his longtime lover Mia Farrow, and her adopted daughter, Soon Yi, will take years to sort out—if ever. The famed actor/director was not the young woman's legal stepfather and denied having been a paternal figure in her life (he did not live with Farrow and her family). But he did admit having had a love affair with her—thereby raising many issues that make us queasy in this era of divorced and reblended families.

The child who sees a stepparent stray—or worse, who is approached sexually by that stepparent—may develop the same kind of intimacy problems as those described above.

Lori's Story

One of my most complex cases involved Lori. She came to me sobbing because she had known for years that her stepfather was cheating on her mother, yet had never told.

Nor had she complained of his flirtatiousness with her. The man—who had married her mother when she was ten years old—watched her hungrily, she said. He would ask her to dance and hold her close, ask her to sit on his lap (she was thirteen years old at the time), and encourage her to wear revealing clothes.

She bolted the bathroom door when she showered, as he often came in without knocking.

But her worst shame, she said, was that she halfway wanted him to see her. She could identify with Mia Farrow's adopted daughter: "That could be me," she said.

Recently, her stepfather had jumped into the shower when she "forgot" to lock the door and began to massage her.

To her horror, she found herself liking it and responding. Involved in a lesbian relationship and declaring herself fearful of men, she feels devastated by both guilt and pleasure.

ADULT SONS OF ADULTEROUS FATHERS

Because of the continuing double standard, adulterous men sometimes boast of their exploits to their male children and may even pass along their mistresses.

John, Randy, and Dan's Stories

That was the case with John. The adult son and grandson of adulterers, he was raised to believe that it was a woman's place to put up with her husband's roving ways. John's wife, Amelia, didn't buy that, and when their five-year-old son asked, "Mommy, are we getting a new Daddy now that Daddy has a new girlfriend?" she laid down the law. Get therapy or get out.

It didn't take much coaxing, for the little boy also appealed to John. "Don't you love Mommy and me anymore?" he asked. "I'll be good, I'll do my homework, I'll go to school."

Randy, in contrast, didn't recognize his legacy, repressing any knowledge of his father's frequent "flings." Then he became involved with Lisa, a coworker. His guilt over the affair tormented him. "Every place I turn, my heart feels heavy, no matter if I'm with my lover or my wife," he told me. "I can't stand the looks on my children's faces." Nevertheless, his dad urged him to divorce his wife, Sheryl, and marry his paramour.

A shocked Randy couldn't understand why until his father came into family therapy. There it emerged that this is what his father wished he'd had the gumption to do years before. "In those days, you didn't get a divorce," he said. Randy still loved Sheryl, though, and decided he was not responsible for fulfilling his father's lost dreams. He also came to realize that he had chosen Sheryl because she was everything he had missed in his father—giving, generous, able to ask for things as neither he nor his father could. Eventually, though, these very traits infuriated him—as often happens when the honeymoon ends.

He deprived her emotionally and materially as he had been deprived and fled into an affair. Through therapy, he came to see that he would keep rerunning this pattern, with a mistress or with other women, until he and his father wrestled with their differences.

No one had a more complicated relationship with his

father than Dan, who bounced back and forth between his lover, Cynthia, and his wife, Suzanne.

Dan's dad had become an irresponsible Romeo relatively late in life, after Dan's vivacious mother, Hannah, died. Every time the little boy started to warm up to a potential stepmother, his father dropped the woman and picked up with another.

Dan swore that he would be eternally faithful and devoted when he married. He then picked a very beautiful and needy woman, Suzanne, the daughter of Holocaust survivors, who was depressed and felt guilty to be alive, like other children of tragic survivors.

Eventually, Dan found it difficult to live with her persistent gloom. He felt inadequate, imprisoned, and pressured. Dan chose an opposite, having never gotten over the loss of his mother, and could not help but miss the joie de vivre Hannah had always brought into her home. He found it in Cynthia.

Given his belief in the sanctity of marriage, though, Dan might have stayed unhappily with Suzanne for years. Cynthia forced the issue, however, asking him to make up his mind. At that point, Suzanne told him he was free to go. She refused to consider therapy to relieve her depression.

In this case, alas, the original marriage could NOT be saved, because Suzanne was not willing to participate in the work needed to do it. She'd rather wallow in misery. When I last saw them, Cynthia and Dan were happily married. I knew that he had been able to successfully rewrite his script.

ADULT SONS OF ADULTEROUS MOTHERS

Because of their own forbidden Oedipal fantasies, many men refuse to admit that their mothers ever had lovers.

Ken's Story

Some respond like Jarrett, whom we have already met, and some like Ken, who became impotent with his girlfriend, Lonnie.

At the age of twelve, Ken had overheard his mother fighting with his beloved surrogate uncle, his father's best friend. The man wanted her to leave and marry him; she refused. The sound of a struggle ensued, a gun went off twice, and his mother screamed for help. Ken rushed to her side and found both his mother and his uncle bleeding. Ken felt doubly betrayed.

His parents later divorced. He buried the trauma deep within. Over the years, he did not allow himself to know why he was always somewhat afraid of his mother and why he blamed her for the divorce.

Lonnie was a warm, loving woman who adored him, but Ken would lose interest in sex or fail to become aroused. He also had violent outbursts of temper.

In therapy, he had to face his anger and work through it to forgive his mom, before he could regain his intimacy with his own lover. Sadly, when his parents, both living alone, came in on the sessions, they wondered rather wistfully whether they might have stayed together if they'd gotten help early enough.

REACHING DEEP INSIDE

Confronting these painful remedies is not easy—but the catharsis is a necessary part of healing.

When Bruce first came to see me, he was ashamed and guilty about the series of one-night stands he'd engaged in while his longtime lover, Mara, was traveling for her new job.

I asked him if this made him feel lonely and if he could remember feeling that way as a youngster. I began to try and guide him into his emptiness.

Suddenly, he WAS that lonely youngster. "Don't leave me!" he wailed. "I feel abandoned when you leave me!"

I urged him to take some deep breaths and continue the

memories. I told him to cry it out, all the pain that had collected over the years. Sobbing, he shouted, "You left me without any warning! One day, I came home and you were *gone* without caring about me."

The message was meant not so much for Mara, it turned out, as for his mother, who'd run away with her lover when he was thirteen. The only time Bruce got his mother to come back was when he used sex to lure her home. He became wildly promiscuous as a teenager, and she returned briefly to bring him into line.

Now he was trying to get Mara's attention with the same tactic. "I miss you so when you're gone, Mara," he said. "I missed my mother. She didn't care and I feel you don't care when you leave."

It was, he said, the first time that he had ever been able to cry about his mother's departure. He and Mara embraced, and she rocked him when I encouraged her. "Tell him what he wanted to hear from his mother," I said. "I love you, I won't leave you again, I am sorry that I abandoned you," she said.

The two then worked out a new compact of understanding. **She promised** to alter her behavior three ways:
- She would ask him to come with her when she traveled, as much as possible.
- She would help and encourage him to express his resentments and loneliness when he felt that way.
- She would try to travel less.

He promised her:
- He would not try to replace her, as he had his mother, with other women.
- He would not use promiscuity to get over the pain of loneliness and
- he would tell her when he missed her.
- He would take an AIDS test.

But the long trek to peace and forgiveness had only begun. I encouraged him to see his mother, Della, whom he hadn't talked to in two years, to deal with his hurt and anger. "If you cut her off, you will never finish the work of your childhood," I said. "Mara will get the fallout, and you will never be happy."

That year, mother and son got together over the Jewish New Year holiday. Della also came to a therapy session, which Mara attended. Tenderly, she held him, and apologized for leaving him. "I should have stayed with your dad. I didn't appreciate him at the time," she said. Not a day had passed, she told him, without her regretting her choice. "Don't ruin your life like I did," she said, urging him to value Mara's love. "You're young, don't follow me." They sobbed together, cradling each other. They both said, "Help me—show me the way."

They helped each other. His mother showed Bruce how to cherish Mara. And Bruce's support encouraged Della to find the strength to leave her abusive second husband.

I have high hopes that this will be a permanent mother-and-child reunion.

The Betrayal Questionnaire

If you have been betrayed, I know it is very difficult for you to do anything other than blame or judge or attack. Look for equal signs, instead. Try to see what family patterns may be at work here. You may be better able to understand the part you played, and move on.

1. Did you suspect your spouse might be unfaithful to you before you married? What were the signs?

2. Did you ever discuss monogamy before you married or moved in together?

3. Did you have a verbal agreement regarding adultery?

4. Do you and your partner believe adultery will or did affect your children?

5. Did your partner's parents or grandparents or did yours commit adultery? What divorces exist in your backgrounds? (See the genogram instructions in the previous chapter.)

6. Is your partner unable to deal with your anger at the affair?

7. Do you want and does your spouse want to save the marriage?

8. Did you or will you give your partner an ultimatum?

9. Is your partner ready to give up the affair?

10. Do you think you played a part in the infidelity? If so, what was it?

A Sin Survey

Early in my research, I asked a random sample of a hundred respondents to tell me their feelings about infidelity.

There were several surprises.

Q. Have your parents or your partner's parents or other members of your family been involved in infidelity?

A. Among those who admitted to having had an affair, 85 percent answered yes to the above question; the rest said they did not know.

Q. Does parental infidelity affect children? If so, how?

A. Every respondent who admitted to having been unfaithful replied yes to this question.

Most said they thought the children would feel "hurt and betrayed."

One man also said, "yes...by example, by setting certain standards as acceptable."

One couple, who declared themselves faithful for seventeen years, replied that children "will absolutely be affected if there is not one-hundred-percent trust between a husband and wife, because the children will sense that."

Q. What would you do if you suspected your spouse had an affair?

A. Overwhelmingly (75 percent) respondents said they would confront the suspected cheater.

Six percent said they would kick the miscreant out of the home.

Only two percent said they would ignore it.

Two women sought special remedies. One said she would kick her mate "in the crotch."

And another, perhaps the cruelest of all, said she would call the IRS.

• 5 •

Running on Empty

By almost any standard, five-year-old Crystal was a lucky little girl. When I met her while I was appearing as a guest expert on "The Oprah Winfrey Show," I could see Crystal was smart, adorable, and blessed with two loving parents.

That was just the problem—and the reason Oprah had invited Crystal's family to appear and ask my advice. Crystal's daddy, Joseph, absolutely doted on her and could deny her nothing—even when she crawled into her parents' bed and wanted to sleep between them all night.

These "sleepovers" made her mother, Denice, feel a tiny bit jealous—and foolish for feeling that way.

But I believe she was justified. As I told both parents, if they don't teach their daughter some boundaries now, there'd be trouble aplenty ahead.

Too many of Daddy's Little Darlings grow up to be Daddy's Big Homewreckers, becoming involved again and again with married men. "She's got to learn it's not okay to come between a couple," I said.

How Our Heartaches Begin: Childhood

One of the most important points I can make is that even the most generous, best-intentioned parents make mistakes that will affect their adult children. As the hugely successful philosopher John Bradshaw has made millions of us understand, we are all wounded children to some degree.

Each of us had some hopes dashed, some talent disparaged, some longing unfulfilled by parents who were no more perfect than any other human beings—despite their godlike dimensions in our eyes.

The noted couples–marital therapist Dr. Harville Hendrix—at whose Institute for Relationship Therapy I trained—explains this accidental damage well. "Even though our parents often had our best interests at heart," he has written, "the overall message handed down to us was a chilling one. There were certain thoughts and feelings we could not have, certain natural behaviors that we had to extinguish, and certain talents and aptitudes we had to deny."

Our parents had unmet childhood needs of their own which they may have passed along to us. And frustrating some childish expectations and needs is part of the socialization process—otherwise, anarchy would rule.

Still, these unheeded needs can cause frustration, hurt, and emotional pain later in life. These feelings chip away at our self-image and cause a yearning at the very center of our beings.

Dr. Thomas Fogarty, my teacher and mentor at the Center for Family Learning, calls this chasm "emptiness." He describes it as **"a black hole—a void of unmet expectations from our family of origin."**

This void is especially deep for those who commit adultery. Their emptiness syndrome starts early, as it does for most of us.

In the normal developmental stages of childhood, for example, infants up to eighteen months are supposed to form strong bonds of attachment to their parents. If their caretakers are not warm and dependably available, however, the babies may develop a fear of abandonment and grow up to be desperate pursuers of love who simultaneously fear intimacy—which is the classic profile of a woman who is betrayed.

Later, between eighteen months and three years, children are supposed to develop a sense of self as they separate from and return to their parents. Overprotection at this stage may produce a fear of absorption, and ultimately result in a **runaway**. This is the typical profile of a male adulterer who seeks a pseudo-intimacy affair.

Similar wounds can occur at any time during our lives, re-enacting our feelings of emptiness. **Among the most seriously wounded children are those who feel abandoned by their mothers and fathers through divorce—or adultery.** If, in addition, they are later betrayed by another loved one—as are so many adult children of adulterers—the anguish may be almost unbearable.

It is useful to think of emptiness in three parts.
- **The emptiness that everyone feels.**
- **The emptiness from not knowing yourself or from losing yourself in another person.**
- **The emptiness that comes from relationships that do not work.**

This gnawing sense of inadequacy, loneliness, and fear is not comfortable to contemplate. We will go to great lengths to avoid confronting it, even failing to discuss it with a psychiatrist during years of therapy. Many of us try to conceal our emptiness by denying it or blocking it out with phoney cheerfulness; some try to bridge it with furious activity or by focusing totally on others.

Most of us mistakenly try to fill it up with alcohol, overeating, workaholism, drugs, or adultery and divorce—which is why there is such an epidemic of affairs.

Infidelity is one of the most common ways of trying to

evade the severe emotional pain we feel when we face the emptiness inside ourselves. You cannot run from it, however. It affects your choice of mate and your ability to enjoy intimacy in your relationships. You must confront and deal with it. One of the secrets of my success in helping couples forgive the unforgivable sin is that I bring in parents, grandparents, and children, so that everyone is forced to take a hard, clear look at their emptiness and its roots in childhood. By so doing, they share their burdens and guide each other. *Emptiness is not as frightening when you confront it with the love and support of others.*

Emptiness often surfaces as a sense of loneliness, isolation, hopelessness, or as an unexplained depression. When those who feel it—but have not acknowledged the feeling—look into their interior mirrors, this is what they see:

"I'm invisible."

Priscilla's parents had a wonderful marriage—so wonderful that they often made her feel nonexistent. Feeling "empty, sad, bored" and losing sexual interest in her husband when she turned thirty, she came to me to try and make her marriage work. Sexual attraction was not really her problem, though; emptiness was. But she would not examine the childhood wounds that had left her feeling so small and insignificant. **That hurt too much.** So she vacillated between her husband and her lover—and both eventually left her.

She did to her husband what her parents did to her—and ended up invisible once again.

"I'm bad."

Lila is also thirty, and another perennial homewrecker. "I want what I cannot have," says Lila, who frequently spills all to the wives of her lovers, without the knowledge or consent of the men. "The badness is that I don't really care about others." She, too, was her father's favorite. She never resolved her attachment to him. He encouraged it because he had a conflicted relationship with her mother. Now she is forever trying to take other men away from their wives.

"I'm unloved."

Ian never really got to know his father, an international airline pilot who was away much of the time. His dad couldn't take Ian out to play catch. He never went to any of his basketball games and didn't even show up at his high-school graduation.

He wasn't much closer to his mother, a beautiful former model and social butterfly who was always flitting off to parties and openings. An unplanned baby and lonely only child, he longed for love, attention, and dependability.

He married Natalie, but never told her of his yearnings. She was shocked to discover he was having an affair. He had to learn to tell her what he needed, and she had to learn to listen.

FALSE IMAGES

Throughout our early childhoods, we also begin to form our image of the Prince or Princess Charming who will someday be our perfect mate. **We piece an ideal together from the positive aspects of both of our parents;** we decide we'll look for someone as strong and funny as our dad and as smart and giving as our mom.

Unconsciously, though, we're also searching for someone with their negative traits as well, so that we can "redo" childhood—and get it right this time! If Mom was overprotective, for instance, we may well be drawn to someone with the same instinct—even though we swore we'd never marry anyone with that trait. The negatives are the strongest part of the attraction. *If we don't find it in our mate, we may look for it in an affair.*

We are setting ourselves up for failure, or at least a rocky road through marriage, as we'll see in chapter 6. Our expectations are just too high. *"People continually try to get from others what they really can only get from themselves, or from themselves what they can only get from a relationship,"* says Dr. Fogarty.

Part of our confusion stems from our own faulty self-image. Growing up, we "lose" the aspects of our personality that our parents don't approve; we're no longer so rambunctious or demanding or blunt. In truth, we don't really lose these traits; we simply hide them behind our public facade. Then along comes someone with those very qualities—and presto, "opposites" attract!

Lars Confronts His Facade

Lars, a civil servant, was having a mid-life crisis—and an affair—at the age of forty-three.

A lonely only child, he'd been raised in an undemonstrative family where affection was rationed as stingily as gifts or money. He married Olga, who was as different as she could be. First he admired, and then came to resent, her outgoing, generous, demonstrative ways.

He took up with a lover who was much more like the facade he presented to the world: repressed and undemanding.

Neither relationship made him happy. "I feel helpless, hopeless, and sad," he said to me.

Although at first he called the prospect of talking to his father and mother about his emptiness "as dangerous as skydiving," he did it. And with a lot of effort on everyone's part, including Olga's, the marriage began to mend.

He realized that deep down, he wished he could ask for things and express his emotions the way she did. Underneath, Lars and Olga were not such opposites after all.

Patty's Lost Paradise

Sometimes a parent can love not wisely but too well. That was the case with Patty.

Her divorced mother bent over backwards to make up to the little girl for the loss of her unfaithful father.

She made Patty the very center of her life. Anything the daughter wanted, the mother gave (thereby alleviating her own emptiness, too). They went sledding in the park, baked brownies in the kitchen, and munched popcorn in front of the TV—always together, of course.

Even when Patty's mother went back to work after the child support stopped, she still managed to always be there for school plays, Girl Scouts, and class trips.

Patty thought she wanted the same nurturing qualities in a husband and figured she'd found them in Chris. But Chris was also building a business and had to work long hours; he didn't have time to re-create Patty's utopia.

Patty turned to an affair with her boss. At first it was wonderful, but then he, too, failed to measure up. No one could match Mama.

Patty came into therapy because she really loved Chris and cared about the marriage. She discovered, however, that her mother's nurturing had been a little bit too much—she had often felt stifled and unable to break away. She learned that, while no man could ever bring back that paradise lost, it wasn't really what she wanted anyway.

THE RELAY RACE OF LOVE

Our emptiness and fixation on images also creates a hidden agenda in our love lives: We become a **pursuer** or a **runaway**, a pattern of alternatives noted by Dr. Fogarty.

EVERY RELATIONSHIP HAS A LOVER AND A BELOVED, A HUNTER AND A HUNTED.

In healthy relationships, the two partners will swap places from time to time. She'll play hard to get, perhaps, and he'll chase after her. It's a harmless, amusing way of preserving excitement, passion, and intrigue. No matter which role each plays, though, they try to stay close enough to touch—but not to disappear into each other.

Adulterers, however, often take these roles to extremes. Many seem to combine the two, becoming sexual hunters and emotional fugitives. However, behind every pursuer is a runaway and behind every runaway is a pursuer.

Many women—I'd estimate 80 percent—are pursuers, trying to fill up their emptiness and complete their selves with the love of another.

The more they love someone, the more they expect this person to "complete" them and provide fulfillment.

Pursuers are frequently suffering from these childhood wounds:
- **abandonment**
- **invisibility**
- **exploitation**
- **being ignored**

Runaways, in contrast, are usually trying to distance themselves from these childhood miseries by fleeing intimacy:
- **smothering**
- **overcontrol**
- **guilt**
- **shame**

About eighty percent of runaways are men. *Forced by society's expectations of masculinity to separate abruptly from their mothers at an early development stage, they may have trouble being intimate with women ever after.* They hope pursuers will rescue them from their loneliness—yet they desperately protect their space. Self-centered, they view relationships as desirable but dangerous and closeness as a sometime thing.

My Father the Runaway

My father was a classic runaway. Whenever my mother pressed too close—hinting about marriage, for example— he'd flee. At one point, he ran all the way to Hollywood, where he dated Ava Gardner and other gorgeous starlets. In that situation, my mother was smart; instead of following, she coolly got on with her life, becoming involved with someone else. Rumors of that fact, of course, brought my father to heel. **Runaways become pursuers when left to their own emptiness.**

For much of her life, though, Mom, like most pursuers, lacked self-esteem. She was the daughter and granddaughter of philanderers; her father never bothered to show up at her high-school graduation because he was detained by his mistress. Subconsciously, she figured she didn't deserve fidelity. It was only after she developed a career of her own and the courage to leave him that my father resolved to be faithful. Even then, it was only after he faced his own inner pain with our help that he was able to keep his promise and we were all able to forgive him fully.

My father was a perfect example of a man in the throes of loneliness. He said to me: "There is not much between me and your mother or between you and your brother. I feel I am more lonely in your presence."

One of the most frequent marital triangles involves a man who flees from too much closeness with his wife, then reverses direction when his mistress demands commitment, too.

Runaway Sam

That was the case with Sam, whom you met in chapter 2. *His wife, Sandra, was a pursuer; she had lost her mother at the age of three and had an unquenchable need for closeness.*

Sam had ambivalent feelings about that. His father had been a traveling salesman who dallied frequently and was never very available to him; his mother was devoted to him. Overly devoted, as it turned out. Sam wanted to escape her smothering, but he also wanted nurture.

When Sandra became overwhelming, he'd turn to Lillian, his mistress. But when she wanted too much cuddling, too much sex—it was back to Sandra.

As noted, what Sam couldn't seem to find in either woman was really himself. Once Sandra stopped pursuing him, he missed her and so he went into his emptiness. What she achieved was more than manipulation, moreover. Because Sam was finally willing to focus on the intimacy problems he'd had since childhood, they were able to get back together and do some real work on their marriage.

Runaway Ryan

Ryan, also from chapter 2, was another runaway who longed for closeness, yet shied away from commitment. When Heidi, a pursuer, one of his two lovers, decided she could live without him, he decided he didn't want to live without her. They are still not married—Ryan doesn't want to do to her what his father did to his mother. But he is no longer taking her for granted, as most runaways do their pursuers. Because she put her foot down, they are trying to overcome their problems.

NOTE: I see with many of my patients that change can begin on one side; even if their mates don't come in for therapy, the betrayed can improve the situation.

Willingness to work is essential if you want to survive adultery. In some ways it is easier to divorce.

None of us wants to recognize the yawning emptiness inside ourselves—it's a dark and scary place. But only when we do can we light it up and clear it out. We can never fill it up or shut it down. But we can acknowledge, accept, and share each other's neediness.

Dan and Debbi Break the Silence

That's what I demonstrated to Dan and Debbi in another appearance on "The Oprah Winfrey Show." This time, the topic was people who hadn't talked to each other for prolonged periods—three months, in their case.

Ostensibly, Debbi wouldn't talk to Dan because he'd crashed their car and been dragged home drunk by the police after an all-night bachelor party at a local "Lingerie Bar."

But as I urged her to look back into her emptiness, other fissures appeared: Her first marriage had ended because her husband got involved with another woman. And further back still, she had felt totally abandoned by her alcoholic mother and father, who left her to be raised in foster homes.

"I felt so alone...I didn't want to lose you," Debbi confessed, choking back the tears.

"I need you. I love you."

By going back to the little girl inside her—with Dan's help—she began to forgive him and to make her marriage heal.

Dan and Debbi never knew it, but they also helped others. I showed the tape of their efforts to Larry, a patient who could not forgive his wife for her betrayal. When he saw Debbi's revelation, he was at last able to understand what his wife felt. **He came to understand, as he saw on "Oprah" that forgiveness is a gift you give yourself.**

Quiz: How Deep Is Your Emptiness?

Frequently, adultery is a desperate attempt to numb the emotional emptiness we feel—that's why the statistics run so high. Everyone gets a little blue, a little down on themselves sometimes. But if you are truly in despair, you may well need counseling.

Ask yourself:

1. Do I feel isolated?
2. Do I feel that I have no one I can talk to?
3. Do I feel this way even when I'm with my partner or my children?
4. Do I feel I am not needed by anybody?
5. Do I feel that I am worthless?
6. Do I feel that things will never change?
7. Do I feel alienated from those close to me?
8. Do I yearn to be taken care of?
9. Do I yearn to be loved?
10. Do I feel shame?
11. Do I feel boredom?
12. Do I feel that nothing matters?
13. Do I feel I am getting older and time is running out?
14. Do I feel like what I hope for, I'll never get?
15. Do I feel like I don't belong anywhere?
16. Do I wish someone really cared about me...just the way I am?
17. Do I feel like a failure?
18. Do I no longer consider myself sexually attractive?
19. Have I lost interest in sex?
20. Do I feel dead inside?

Give yourself 2 points for each **Yes** answer. If you have a score of 8 or more, you are experiencing the emptiness syndrome. If you or your spouse answers yes to most of these questions, you are vulnerable to an affair—and you should seek help to alleviate your pain.

Troubled Waters

But love is blind, and lovers cannot see the
pretty follies that they themselves commit.
　　　　　—William Shakespeare

Remember how it felt when you first fell in love? Your
heart leapt up and your pulse raced when you beheld your
beloved. All you could see was perfection: You couldn't get
enough of each other's company, nor talk about each other
sufficiently in the rare moments you were apart.

Unfortunately, **it's not only Hollywood screenwriters
who,** in their invented worlds, **believe you can and should
sustain that period of breathless infatuation forever.**

Lots of us still dream of the endless honeymoon and
wonder why this romantic season so often ends with a thud.

How the Honeymoon Ended for Janice and Len

When Janice and Len were dating, for example, she
treasured his free-spirited ways, while he was proud of her

fashion sense. For their first three months of marriage, all was well; he brought her flowers, she always looked great.

But then his disdain for routine began to annoy her: He forgot to call when he'd be late for dinner; he disappeared with his buddies when her parents came to visit.

Her clothes-consciousness wore thin, too: the credit-card bills were enormous; she spent hours getting ready.

They started to snipe, and then to argue; she'd complain; he'd retreat in injured silence.

As with any couple, after those first delirious months they were quarreling about power.

They needed to learn to communicate and negotiate effectively to pass through these shoals and reach the promised land: the full and flexible intimacy that I call **Real-Life Love**.

EVERY RELATIONSHIP MOVES INTO A POWER STRUGGLE ONCE THE HONEYMOON IS OVER.

But the inevitable disillusionments that set in as a relationship matures don't have to be destructive. You don't have to flee into silence, affair, or divorce; you can stay and repair your relationship.

Those who can't or won't deal with their own emptiness—and the false expectations they bring to a relationship—never reach that high ground of Real-Life Love. Too often, they turn to an extramarital partner as a way to relive those first passionate days and escape conflict.

That's not an effective answer, however—they risk being stuck at that stage, only to repeat the same mistakes over and over again in every new relationship. (One of the reasons that the level of adultery and divorce rises with every remarriage is that people may change partners, but they still take their problems with them.)

Passage through the stages and stress points of a marriage

is extraordinarily difficult. If you watch out for certain perils, however, you can better your chances of making it through.

STAGE ONE: THE HONEYMOON STAGE

The honeymoon always carries the seeds of its own destruction. As we saw in the last chapter, we're all looking for someone who will help us finish the unresolved issues of our early years. That usually means, however, that we marry the person who will give us the most trouble. **We want to redo the negative traits of our parents as well as re-create the positive ones, and we're attracted to those who have many of the traits we disowned as children.**

Thus pursuers are attracted to runaways. My mother, who mourned her father's infidelity, went right ahead and married a playboy, convinced that "I can change him." Full of such delusions, we fail to notice the negative aspects of our mates clearly during courtship—only to recoil when they appear later. **What attracted you then, repulses you now.**

When they were still lovers, for instance, Sal was delighted that Gina was so uninhibited in bed. Once they married, though, he found it unseemly—especially after the baby was born. Soon he was seeking his sexual pleasure elsewhere.

Like a lot of men, he suffered from the Madonna/Whore complex; he wanted sex with the latter, but marriage with the former. He had to learn that, yes, a woman can be a mom and still be interested in oral sex!

The complex cuts both ways; Shari was hot for Darren before they married, but lost her desire once they wed; call hers a stud/spouse complex.

While the honeymoon can't run forever, you *can* recapture some of its joys. Remember to regularly renew the excitement by scheduling time for each other; try hot tubs, massages, sexy lingerie, candlelight-and-champagne suppers, or whatever pleases your passion. This will help you bond and master the next inevitable stage—the power struggle.

None of us really wants to leave this floating, dreamy time, which is a throwback to infancy when all our needs were met. **An affair replicates the mindless honeymoon madness. Replicate it in your marriage or relationship instead. Periodically, we need to remind ourselves of why we loved and chose our mates in the first place.**

No-Passion Pairings

As many problems as passion can cause honeymooners, its absence is even worse for the marriage. I'm concerned about the increasing number of men and women in the No-nonsense Nineties who seem to skip the honeymoon stage entirely. Instead of marrying for love, they seem to settle down for practical or status reasons: They want to have kids, and time is ticking away; they want to upgrade their security, and acquire status with a rich/powerful/gorgeous spouse; they want to settle down in their own home; or they're tired of dating and afraid of AIDS.

Few of us, though, are really that hardheaded—or hard-hearted. **While you can't fuel a marriage on passion alone, that's what gets you through troubled waters. In my experience, those who marry without love will eventually look elsewhere—and move on.** They lack the glue that will keep them together and carry them through the traumatic changes ahead.

Take Linda, a thirty-nine-year-old newscaster who relished her career but began to hear the alarm ringing on her biological clock. Reproached constantly by her family: "When are you going to get married and start a family? We want grandchildren...it will soon be too late!"—she decided to cast around for the best available talent.

Matt, forty-one, seemed the right fit; he, too, was successful, good-looking, and well educated, with a top job in advertising...and he welcomed being seen with a celebrity like Linda.

Both convinced themselves they were right for each other. They weren't in love with each other, though—only with the IDEA of love. After the excitement of their engagement and wedding, however, they found themselves alone, with no one else to admire their perfection—and things fell apart.

One year later, both were having affairs. And within two years of the wedding, they were divorced.

Bart, thirty-one, also married for the wrong reasons. While in medical school, he hitched himself to Nancy, thirty-three, a nurse, because he wanted someone to take care of him, cook his meals, help with rent. Nancy, whose mother had recently died, was lonesome and wanted to feel needed again.

The marriage survived until he finished school, started his practice, and began making money. He soon felt stifled by her nurturing. Sadly, in a pattern that's still all too common among professional men, he dumped her when he fell in love with an intern whose dad was a chief-of-staff at his hospital.

STAGE TWO: THE POWER STRUGGLE

IT'S BOUND TO HAPPEN. ONE DAY YOU LOOK UP, AND INSTEAD OF SEEING SOME ENCHANTING STRANGER ACROSS A CROWDED ROOM YOU SEE A FLAWED FAMILIAR ON THE OTHER SIDE OF A MESSY KITCHEN.

Time for reality to set in: kids, deadlines, bills, chores, different notions of punctuality, neatness, civility. Incompatabilities appear. Desires and needs clash. I want you to give me what my father never did; you want the same from me.

Face it: now you are A COUPLE. Each of you experiences some **redefinition**: who am I as half of a *pair*? What do *I* want that he's willing to give? How far will I go to meet *his* needs?

Some run from these questions and commitments into another's arms, where they can sink back into the bliss of a honeymoon. "It's more threatening for me to have sustained intimacy with my spouse than only 'moments' in an affair," explained one of my male patients.

That's pretty shortsighted, though. **Unless you plan to indulge endlessly in one-night stands—pretty difficult and dangerous in the age of AIDS—your affair will lurch into the power-struggle stage sooner or later due to that big "C" word—commitment.**

That's why so few adulterous spouses wind up leaving their mates for their lovers—five to ten percent in the experience of many therapists, and two percent in mine.

"She's acting just like my wife!"

Consider the case of Harris, a pharmacist, who left his wife, Anita, for Joan, a cosmetic company representative. When he came to see me at Anita's urging, he said she was just too bossy. She wanted everything her own way, just as his mother had. "My wife never let me choose a show or a restaurant," he said. Joan, in contrast, was ideal: "*Anything* I want is okay with Joan."

I was not entirely surprised, however, when he came back six months later to grouse that now the reverse was true. "Joan keeps tabs on all my movements," he complained. Not only that, but "I wanted to go to an Italian restaurant last night and she insisted we go to a new Japanese one. She's acting just like my wife!"

Another honeymoon over.

I told him his main problem was that he didn't clearly

assert his wants and needs. Instead of blaming either of the women in his life, he had to stand up for himself—as he'd never learned to do with his mother.

Harris opted to go through this struggle with Anita rather than Joan. "I have a history with my wife and two children at home," he said.

If you don't handle your childhood conflicts, it's just a matter of time before a lover begins to look more and more spouselike or parentlike. If you change partners during this tumultuous stage instead of changing yourself and your relationship, you still won't find what you want.

This period of adjustment is difficult, but it can also bring excitement and commitment back to a relationship—and even inspire its own brand of ardor. *Kissing and making up IS fun,* just as those old wives' tales always said—how else do you think the storytellers got to be old wives in the first place?

Opening Up the Communication Shutdown

Many marriages stagnate in the power-struggle stage because the partners are too polite for words. Diane and Dale, for instance, were high-school sweethearts who never fought, but who rarely made love, either.

In what I believe was an attempt to rescue his marriage, he created a crisis by having an affair that he knew Diane would hear about.

Sure enough, she did, and that brought the two of them to me. They had to learn how to fight fair (see chapter 9, for the rules on fighting fair). They began to share the fears instilled by their perfectionist parents. And they learned to laugh as well as cry together.

Today, they're enjoying the third stage of marriage because they were willing to engage themselves in the effort.

As Barbara De Angelis states in her book *Are You the One For Me?,* "Remember, falling in love is the easy part, but building a healthy relationship takes hard work."

STAGE THREE: REAL-LIFE LOVE

I was brought up to believe that love is easy. That anyone related by blood naturally loved other family members, and that when the time was right, I would fall in love and naturally know what to do to develop that love. I now know that love is very difficult.

John Bradshaw, *Creating Love*

Bradshaw is right.

Very few partners are willing to dig through the secret emptiness inside, identify their needs and convey them to their parents as well as their partners. We are too lazy, scared, or tired. Instead, we change partners or opt for loneliness.

Undeniably, Real-Life Love may take a long time to achieve: thirty-five years, in my parents' case. And, as we've seen, many never manage this at all.

But those who do, know a rare fulfillment.

In this stage, your love is tested and tempered like steel. Your relationship is not static—you renegotiate the terms of your marriage as both of you change and grow.

This is not a second honeymoon; both partners are wiser and more clear-eyed than that. They have learned to share goals; they know that helping a mate satisfy his or her needs can satisfy their own as well. If my lack of punctuality has always driven you nuts, I may resolve to reform, knowing that will not only make you happy but please me, too, as I increase my sense of self-mastery.

Often, as we've seen, partners turn to adultery in an *ineffective* attempt to finish their childhood behavior. Marriage offers an *effective* way to do this, achieving self-realization as well as mutual happiness.

The Cara Mia Contract

Consider clever Margarita. Her husband, Frank, went into a mid-life panic when the promotion he'd wanted went to a younger man. His hair thinning, his paunch expanding, he sought an ego boost by becoming entangled with his beautiful young assistant.

His wife, Margarita, was also beautiful, but charming, too, and well liked by her acquaintances. So when Frank squired his new sweetheart to restaurants where the couple had always gone, loyal staff passed on the word.

One evening, when the lovebirds were dining, the sommelier brought over a bottle of Frank's favorite champagne, and said it was from an admirer. The attached note said simply, "love, Cara Mia."

It was his pet name for Margarita.

Frank rushed through dinner and hurried home.

There she greeted him in an elegant negligee and simply said, "Let's talk."

They did—for six hours. He told her for the first time about his own emptiness and loneliness. She told him about her own emptiness now that the children were gone.

She also conveyed how he had hurt her by turning to someone else—and she made him vow that he would never do so again.

He has kept that vow, and their marriage has never been better. *They survived the power struggle and made it work for them.*

STRESS POINTS

No matter what stage your marriage is in, it can be rocked by periods of transition. When we hit one of these rough spots, our emptiness asserts itself and we're especially vulnerable to affairs.

In many cases, as I've noted, transitional affairs are a desperate attempt to fend off change and reassert the status quo. Like Frank, the adulterer may be hoping to relieve his anxieties without disrupting his marriage.

Breakups at these bumpy points are frequent but not inevitable—as Margarita demonstrated.

Just remember: *All relationships are fragile, especially at these times—so try to be especially forthcoming with your mate.*

The Seven Deadliest Stress Points

1. Having a baby

The impending arrival of a child due to pregnancy or adoption awakens many of our sleeping demons. A partner may fear and resent the intruder, remembering how he felt when a sibling appeared to elbow him aside. A father or even a mother-to-be may panic: *"I'm not ready to grow up and be a mom/dad!"*

Margie was so thrilled to discover that she was two months pregnant after several miscarriages that she failed to notice that Paul didn't share her delight.

Given her previous experience, Margie was exceedingly careful. She required a great deal of bed rest and was afraid to have sex.

Since both were intimacy avoiders, she didn't tell him of her fears. He was too selfish to notice. He took up with her best friend, because his childhood resentments came rushing back. He remembered how his parents had gurgled over his baby sister and ignored their shy, scholarly son, and he feared a rerun. Although she was devastated, Margie worked very hard in therapy to save her marriage. The only problem was that Paul preferred the "feel-good" affair to working on problems in therapy, so she had to leave him.

Sometimes, pregnancy is a misguided effort to glue a marriage back together. **It can also backfire into an affair**.

Denise and Earl, residents at a large hospital, used work, fatigue, and dalliances to keep their distance from each other; both had affairs with others. She realized their love couldn't go on like that and deliberately became pregnant. He became furious, and they opted for counseling.

2. Mid-life

This is an equal-opportunity crisis, striking women as well as men.

Darlene and Don had always avoided conflict. They'd wed when she was eighteen—partly because she felt so lonely while her parents worked late nights at their grocery store. Eventually, Darlene inherited the store and Don ran it. That troubled her; the late nights reminded her of her childhood isolation.

When she tried to join Don at the store, however, he dismissed her suggestions. Her neighbor, Lou, was not dismissive, though; they engaged in wonderful chats about local politics whenever they met at parties. Soon they were engaged in something more. "He noticed when I went to the beauty parlor and had my hair done," Darlene explained. "He admired my ability to evaluate political candidates. He thought I was someone special."

3. Job loss

Many of us have tied our self-esteem to our job status and when we fail at that, everything seems to break down.

So it was with Marvin, who was badly shaken when his dress factory failed during the recession. Formerly wealthy and powerful, he couldn't bear the humiliation of bankruptcy. He'd always been his own boss, but when he forced himself to look for jobs, they kept telling him he was overqualified.

Marvin, 53, knew that was a codeword for old.

His self-esteem plummeted. *It was just like the sudden dive he'd taken when his brother arrived sixteen years after he was born.* He'd never forgotten that pain; now he tried to relieve it by dallying with the attractive headhunter who was helping him look for work.

4. Bereavement

Death reminds us of all the conflicts left unsettled, the closeness that might have been. It also, of course, underscores our own mortality.

Derek, a forty-year-old stockbroker, was hard hit when his father died. Although he loved his dad deeply, he'd never discussed his father's affair or forgiven him for it. He acted out his anger by identifying with his father.

Shortly after the funeral, Derek pursued a fellow broker— and caught her. His wife, Kim, was humiliated when she found out through Wall Street gossip. He loved Kim deeply, however, and when he managed to grieve for his father and forgive his betrayal, only then was Derek able to end the affair and move on to Real-Life Love.

The death of a child can be even more devastating.

When Myrna and Stan's sixteen-year-old son, Lyle, died in a motorcycle accident, they were injured emotionally. She blamed Stan for allowing their boy to have a motorcycle. They were too stricken by this tragedy even to discuss it, and they separated with no resolution after he had a brief affair.

5. Illness/Serious Conditions

Serious conditions or illnesses often strain relationships, and we may feel guilty about admitting that.

Josh and Carol both loved Josh, Jr., but he was a very demanding child. Hyperactive, he whirled around the house day and night. Carol devoted herself thoroughly to his care, which included a special diet, exercises, and constant vigilance.

Josh felt neglected and guilty that he had somehow failed the boy and himself. His parents had expected him to be a model in everything—how could he be a model father with a son like that?

He fled into an affair.

6. Parental divorce

This can rock us almost like a death, especially if we fear it may be "catching" in some way. (In fact, I have seen it reverberate in the behavior of family members, who get divorced themselves.)

Regina was thunderstruck by the news that her folks were getting a divorce after thirty years. Angry at her father for initiating the separation, she acted it out by becoming involved with an older man. She scattered a lot of obvious clues around, however, practically begging to be caught. When she was, the whole family entered therapy. She and her husband eventually reconciled—and so did her parents.

7. Change in status

Sometimes, it's retirement, as it was for Regina's father. Often, it's a wife's return to work after several years off to take care of the kids. I still remember how my own father reacted when my mother decided in her late thirties to open an antiques store. One day when I was at the store, he called and told her she had to come home right away.

The problem? He was trying to make a tuna fish sandwich for himself and couldn't even figure out how to open the can.

She told him how to do that and how to make the salad— over the telephone. The next day, he not only made his own sandwich, he brought her one.

They still hadn't solved their underlying troubles, though—and Dad was soon enmeshed in another affair.

Once you're aware of how and why problems separate two people you can look at them squarely. It's the first of many difficult but doable steps.

• 7 •

Facing the Facts

When Shari put on her exercise tape at 6:15 one morning, she got more of a workout than she bargained for. Instead of Jane Fonda, as expected, there was her husband, Leon, cavorting naked with a saleswoman from his real estate office.

The other woman was wearing a red lace Merry Widow, garter belt, and heels. Worse, the duo was doing an enthusiastic mutual rendition of oral sex—something Leon had never been willing to try with her!

That was certainly the most dramatic clue to a mate's indiscretions that any of my patients ever received. (Leon had *"accidentally"* left his homemade tape mixed in with Shari's videos.) Still, even if they are usually more subtle, most partners do provide plenty of hints to their wanderlust, as we've seen.

I don't believe affairs "just happen." And I don't believe they happen without warning. If the warning signals had been heeded, in most cases the affair would have been stopped or even prevented. Discovery usually turns out to be verification rather than new information. In the majority of cases, the partner unconsciously knows or suspects— just as children do. This does NOT mean, however, that the betrayed person should assume the entire burden for the situation.

I do not buy the excuse made by many adulterous men and women: "I wouldn't have done this if you hadn't driven me to it!"

But if deceived mates don't drive the deceiver to adultery, they usually give him/her permission to go there—and even carfare. Like the spouse of an alcoholic, the philanderer's partner is a sort of codependent who enables the behavior to continue by denying or ignoring warning signs.

Both sides play a part. We've got to face two hard facts about infidelity:

- **A partner who feels dissatisfied but doesn't convey that feeling is looking for trouble.**
- **A partner who doesn't listen to what the other partner is saying is asking for trouble, too.**

DRAWING THE LINE

Like Margarita in the previous chapter, marriage survivors know how to establish behavioral boundaries, define them clearly, and enforce them.

You and your partner must decide for yourselves how much latitude you want to allow. Forget about what society or your cleric says is immoral. What do you two believe?

You must discuss your beliefs about monogamy and fidelity before you marry or share a home, and you must review them every once in a while during your marriage.

Where do YOU draw the line? Here are some benchmarks to help you decide.

FANTASY

Maybe we shouldn't have laughed at Jimmy Carter when he confessed to "lusting in his heart." **In 1986, when *People***

magazine polled its readers on what unfaithfulness meant to them, a surprising 21 percent declared that just thinking about sex with someone other than their true love was wrong.

Still, the majority of Americans accept that it's normal to fantasize occasionally. Most of us understand that our partners sometimes dream about some singer or movie star—even if we don't want to hear all about it, especially at intimate moments!

The question becomes trickier, though, if your partner experiences pangs of passion for someone closer to hand.

That's what Bob discovered when he made the serious mistake of telling Elaine, his longtime girlfriend, that he fancied one of the other single women who shared their weekend ski house.

If he'd stopped there, it might not have been so bad, but he drooled on in lascivious detail. Already afraid of intimacy, she felt stabbed by a knife in the heart.

In therapy, Bob made a different discovery: Sometimes it IS possible to communicate too much. He came to realize that honesty can be cruel—his honesty was not as innocent as it seemed. *He admitted that he was testing her love; he wanted her to stop him as a way of showing how much she cared.* She came to a realization, too—that joining a house full of attractive single women was her way of avoiding suffocation. Talk about asking for trouble.

Those who are feeling dangerously drawn to another might try confiding less graphically. Tell a mate that you're depressed, or lonely, or feeling excluded. Then try something along these lines: "I don't want to have an affair. I feel like doing it, although I won't. I feel like a failure. I miss you when you're spending so much time on work, baby, etc. I feel very vulnerable. I need something; I need you."

FLIRTATION

When you begin to act out your fantasies by flirting with someone, have you gone too far?

This has always been an explosive question—ask any long-married couple how many fights can start after a neighborhood barbecue or cocktail party.

These days, the tension runs higher than ever: One man's "innocent joke" may be another woman's sexual harassment, especially in a work-related setting. Men and women often feel very differently about this situation, as the reactions to the Clarence Thomas/Anita Hill hearings demonstrated.

The only solution is for partners to hammer out what THEIR ground rules are. For example:

- Is it O.K. to bat your eyelashes or gaze raptly into another's eyes, but wrong to dance close?
- Is it permissible to flirt if your mate's not present, but impermissible otherwise? Or vice versa?

Couples who always spend their time at parties apart, cozying up to others, may not be getting what they want from each other. Persistent, pronounced flirtatiousness is not just casual or innocent—it's a warning sign. *Remember, adultery doesn't just happen.*

Try to set your rules early in a relationship, and remind yourself: **If ONE partner thinks there's a problem, there's a problem.**

FRIENDSHIP

Most of us believe that it IS possible to have a friendship with a member of the opposite sex, even if we don't think it's probable.

But it is all too easy for friendship to get too friendly. And now that a majority of women work outside the home, the temptations are enormous. Male and female colleagues lunch together, work late on projects together, travel on business trips together. All perfectly aboveboard—yet who among us has not felt those old familiar jealous twinges when we hear about the witty remark that Jennifer made at the sales meeting or Lew's unbelievable tennis serve?

Don't sweep these feelings under the rug. Talk about them.

Make no mistake, more than half the men and women who commit adultery meet their lovers at the workplace.

If you feel your mate may be putting himself or your relationship in danger by spending so much time with an office pal, discuss it. *You can communicate your feelings and set limits without sounding paranoid—and you can erect a stop sign that will help you both to define your boundaries.*

AFFAIRS OF THE HEART

DAY-TO-DAY FRIENDSHIPS CAN TURN INTO THE ENTAN-GLING RELATIONSHIPS WE CALL AFFAIRS OF THE HEART. THEY CAN BE DEVASTATING.

Consider Merle and Marty. He thought Merle was over-reacting to all the time he was spending with her sister, Cindy. Hey, they had so much to talk about: He was an architect and she was an interior decorator. So what if they sat on the beach together freezing Merle out or stayed up all night talking? It was absolutely, strictly platonic...Cindy was a great girl.

"I sat there like the invisible woman," said Merle, a stunning fashion designer. "Maybe it would have been better if they *had* slept together. I can compete with that. But I can't match her knowledge about his business. They're kindred spirits. She was always smarter than me." She was deeply distressed by this emotional betrayal, because it reinforced childhood hurts. Once again, Merle was coming in second to her sister.

These emotional liaisons can be very, very dangerous, even if they don't proceed to sex. Those who are bound to another emotionally are often harder to break apart than those whose only involvement is physical. In such cases, the wanderer often winds up marrying the lover.

Think about it: If you're pouring time and emotional energy into this relationship, do you have enough left over for your primary partner?

Eric definitely didn't. A biochemist, he became very friendly with Martine, a research associate, while both were completing their doctorates. They were also great tennis companions.

Still, Eric's wife, Zelda, wasn't worried. She knew she was far more attractive than the short, overmuscled Martine, and besides, their sex life was *hot*.

But several months later, she came into my office weeping bitterly. Eric wanted a divorce to marry Martine. They'd never slept together, as he was fiercely opposed to infidelity. But he said she offered qualities that Zelda couldn't match: her intellectual gifts, her athleticism. Zelda had been there for him when he was suffering through the trials of his doctoral effort. She knew what he was going through.

Eric and Zelda reconciled, but only after he saw what he had been reluctant to admit to himself: how much he needed his wife. His involvement with Martine was an effort to distance himself from his wife, to disguise his vulnerability.

THE GALAHAD TEMPTATION

Noble intentions often spark affairs. When you ride to the rescue of a friend like Sir Galahad or Florence Nightingale, you may be tempted to offer more than a shoulder to cry on.

Witness what happened to Carol and Jason and their good friend, Vivian.

Caught up in her career, Carol asked her husband to devote some time to cheering up the newly widowed Vivian. He'd drop by regularly, to pitch in with picture hanging or tax preparation, or just to chat; he admired her courage, and tried to keep her from despondency.

Carol, meanwhile, seemed oblivious to how much time the widow and her spouse were spending together.

When Jason and Carol embarked on a vacation cruise, it seemed only natural to invite Vivian along. Carol was seasick for much of the trip, however, and by the time the trio returned to home port, Jason and Vivian were deeply involved lovers.

Carol had allowed a dangerous situation to develop; she had all but pushed Jason over the line. Her desire to be a generous friend backfired.

In such situations, the straying spouse often finds it more difficult than usual to end the affair. "I can't hurt this needy person at such a difficult time," is the rationalization. Tracy, for example, grew close to her coworker, Harry, after he was badly injured in a car accident. She visited him regularly, patiently helping him with exercises to bring back his memory and his speech.

When he was released, he showed his gratitude by taking her out to a romantic dinner without her husband, Gil. Matters escalated, and soon they were having a steamy affair.

She felt little guilt, though, because she was making Harry feel better. As the song says, "STOP—IN THE NAME OF LOVE."

If you suspect a friendship has turned into a love affair, or threatens to do so, what should you do? **Don't ask open-ended questions such as, "Are you having an affair?"** (Your mate can simply say no, without discussion.) Say, **"I know you are having an affair," or "I know you are thinking of having a fling with so-and-so."** Speak affirmatively!

You don't have to collude in adultery. If you discuss the affair—or the temptation to have one—immediately and candidly, there is more chance of stopping it even if it has begun. In many of the emotional liaisons, clues are left because, yes, the adulterer *does* want to be stopped.

How to Hold That Line

Oscar Wilde once opined that the only way to get rid of temptation was to yield to it, but remember: He ended up in jail.

Once you've established your boundaries, there are ways to patrol them and to minimize the threats from without and within.

IF YOU ARE THE ONE WHO FEELS TEMPTED:

Ask yourself what you see in the other person that you cannot or do not get from your mate. Then ask your mate whether he or she would and could meet those needs.

If the attraction is purely physical, try to imagine your target ten years older and twenty pounds heavier.

Make a list of the person's annoying habits: Biting nails or smoking. (This skips the honeymoon stage and takes you straight to the power struggle!)

Look at this negative list three times a day.

Draw up a list of the things you love about your mate.

Look at this positive list three times a day. Tell your mate what's on this love list—and encourage more of the same!

Remember: Meeting encourages cheating. If you're trying to fight an attraction to someone—or you don't want to develop one—avoid the following:

- Don't go on a pub crawl with the gang...unless you bring your spouse. It's not for naught that most country songs about cheating take place in honky-tonks and bars. Alcohol lowers inhibitions.
- Don't lunch alone with your friend all the time—invite some others along.
- Don't be the last to leave a party or business dinner with this person and don't offer a ride home.

Talk positively about your spouse to your friend. Com-

plaints don't count—and if you both start talking about your
rotten sex lives at home, you're hooked.

If permitted, **invite your partner** along to social and
business functions such as overnight conventions, Christmas
parties, and outings. If not, have him/her pick you up at the
office, and make introductions to your special pal.

IF YOU ARE THE BETRAYED:

Don't share your mate. It's fine to lend a hand to a
deserving friend...but since four hands are even better, why
don't you go along?

Don't sulk at home. If evening entertaining or cocktails is
part of your partner's business, make it part of yours, too.

Keep up with your mate's business and other interests.

Ask what new sexual techniques your partner would like to
try...and tell him or her your secret desires.

Plan frequent outings together without the kids. Try
activities you know the other person likes.

When you are apart, **communicate** meaningfully. Don't
limit yourself to perfunctory phone calls. Talk for at least ten
minutes a day.

If he/she's going to be on the road for a long time, **tuck a
tape** of your voice reading their favorite books or poems into
their luggage.

Make sure your mate has a current, flattering picture of
you for the office...and maybe some fun snapshots, too.

If you're hearing more than you care to about some
paragon colleague, **invite** the person along to a dinner or
party, so you can check the competition firsthand.

When you do meet potential rivals, establish your turf.
Dress up! Be affectionate—put your arm around your mate.
Make some inside jokes or refer to some times you've shared
together.

• 8 •

Situational Sex

Is adultery ever O.K.? Is it acceptable under certain circumstances?

Sean and Cassie certainly seemed to think so. During the two years they lived together in the early eighties, they were enthusiastic members of a sexual swingers' club. "I had always been curious, and I didn't see it as wrong," says Cassie, a twenty-six-year-old graphic artist. "I saw it as a way to keep the relationship exciting. I didn't want somebody to get used to me and cheat."

But then she actually married Sean, an accountant, and became concerned about AIDS and about raising children. Sean was furious that she wanted to end their wild ways. "She agreed that we were going to have variety in our marriage, and now she's backed out," he fumed.

Eventually, they divorced, and Cassie is still trying to get over her hurt and distrust through therapy. She now understands she picked a mate who represented her conflicting desires for closeness and distance. She knows she could not find in the arms of other men the warmth lacking in her

95

father during childhood. Now she's looking for a healthy, committed relationship.

I can't remember ANY case in my many years of practice where someone was not hurt by infidelity, whether it was the betrayer, the betrayed, or their child. That's why I firmly believe in fidelity.

ADULTERY IS NEVER O.K.

I don't like to make highhanded moral judgments—we're all too imperfect for that. But I do know that it is *not* permissible to hurt someone you love or to pass along that hurt to your blameless children.

Anytime you use someone else to put distance between your partner and yourself—whether it is through swinging, a sexual affair, or an emotional entanglement—there is something you are avoiding in your relationship and yourself.

Danger of Affairs

These days, of course, there is another crucial reason to avoid extramarital involvements. You might hurt someone permanently. Sexually transmitted diseases (STDs), such as chlamydia and herpes, can inflict infertility as well as lasting physical and emotional pain.

New York matrimonial lawyer Barbara Bevando Sobal notes that one out of five sexually active adults now has or has had an STD. "Each partner takes the risk of not only having a sexual encounter with that person, but also with a possible unknown army that includes all past lovers," she says. This stark reality makes infection a frequent cause for divorce. In some states, she adds, knowing transmission of an STD is classed as a crime.

When the disease passed along is AIDS, of course, it can kill. Currently, the rate of women infected through hetero-sexual intercourse rose 43 percent between 1990 and 1991.

"AIDS is increasingly becoming a disease of women, of heterosexuals, of the young, and of families," warns former U.S. Surgeon General Antonia Novello. I myself have seen several AIDS cases among my patients, and now that an estimated one million Americans are affected with HIV, I'm sure I will see more.

I will never erase the memory of Veronica and Kyle, whom you met in chapter 1. They did not marry once it was discovered that he had passed along his HIV to her. He remains symptomless; she is dying. They remain together as caretaker and patient, locked in by fury and guilt.

Whenever I appear on television or give a speech, I'm always asked questions that qualify adultery: Is it ever per-missible—even beneficial? Is a one-night stand all right if you are not in love with the person? If you love your spouse and you're just doing it for sexual satisfaction? If you don't tell? If you do?

My answer is always the same. I don't believe in situational sex. Why? Because, over time, an extramarital affair will not work. The deep pain and intimacy problems it reflects will not go away. They will surface eventually...in another generation.

I know—because my patients tell me—that some therapists advise their clients that affairs can be purely recreational and help marriages survive by stabilizing them. That's not my experience, however, nor was it the experience of Yvette.

This depressed young woman spent thirteen years with an analyst who kept assuring her that her husband Don's sexual escapades were perfectly permissible. Do your own thing, he urged her. He's just being a man; if it bothers you, sleep in separate bedrooms.

She eventually discovered that the therapist was a real Lothario himself, carrying on in his penthouse apartment while his wife lived sedately on another floor in the same building.

She and Don then came to see me. I was appalled by the callous advice they'd been given. It took six years to undo the aftereffects, but they're finally back in the same bed— exclusively.

Like many of the betrayed, Yvette suffered from low self-esteem. Raised to do what she was told, she tried to go along with the therapist's advice, then wondered what was wrong with her when she couldn't take Don's adultery in stride. She accepted the notion that affairs were permissible because she didn't value herself enough to demand fidelity.

She needed to stand up for herself, conquer her fear of abandonment, and learn to say no!

You deserve more, and you'll get more, as did my mother and many of my patients.

Special Circumstances

Let's take a careful look at some other instances that supposedly make affairs O.K.

MUTUAL CONSENT

Years after the publication of *Open Marriage*, a 1972 best-seller by Nena and George O'Neill, some people still support their argument that sexual fidelity is "the false god of closed marriage."

Theoretically, if both mates want to swing, or swap, or openly sleep around, who am I to say it's wrong?

But in practice this rarely turns out to really be a true free choice for both partners. **In my experience, in almost all cases, one partner acquiesces out of fear of losing the other. The reluctant player is coerced or humiliated or teased into participating** when a spouse says, "What's wrong with it? Don't be so possessive! Everyone else is doing it."

That happened to two couples—Joe and Mary, Jim and Anne—who tried mate-swapping one night as a lark when they were all stranded in the same hotel room during a vacation.

They all liked the sensation, or said they did, and were soon swapping regularly.

But Joe came to me because he wanted to stop. Mary didn't, exactly. She fell in love with Jim and wanted a permanent switch. The subsequent divorces left Joe and Alice to go their separate, bitter ways. They didn't form a new couple, together, and the friendship of twenty years between Jim and Joe was also shattered. Yes, Jim and Mary married— but one wonders how long that union will last.

On paper and perhaps in other cultures, sharing a marriage partner may seem logical, but in reality, it is destructive. **I have never seen sharing or swapping work. In every case I've seen the relationship broke up.** An open marriage is usually an indication that one or the other partner fears commitment. Sooner or later, one or the other will want to get off the merry-go-round, as both Joe and Cassie did.

As for jealousy, I think a moderate amount is healthy and necessary. Real-Life Love only comes from a committed relationship. Only through monogamy can you complete your childhood, survive the power struggle, and find true happiness, growth, and healing.

Even in the rare cases where the choice is truly mutual, it's dysfunctional.

Brian and Karen were a splendid-looking couple, she an assistant TV producer, he an ad salesman. Both were also the adult children of adulterous parents. He encouraged her to go out dancing with other men, have sex with them, and then come home and make love to him (although he didn't swing himself).

By some strange logic, they felt this gave them control over their legacy of adultery. "I like the idea that after other guys went for her, she would be coming home to me," he said. "It turns me on." (An extreme homophobe, he never considered the idea that he was also expressing his own latent homosexuality.)

Allegedly, this situation made them both happy. But then they decided to adopt a baby. They came to me to find out what to tell the child and what effect their behavior might have on it.

After several sessions, they decided not to adopt. I think it was a wise decision. Children express what their parents suppress. Given this volatile situation, kids will grow up with confusion about sexual constancy, identity, and intimacy— especially adopted kids, who are already coping with questions about abandonment and where they belong.

Any time partners need a third—or fourth or fifth—party to keep their relationship going, it's because they're afraid to face intimacy with each other.

For all those reasons, **open marriage is a closed issue.**

DISABILITY

When one partner is ill or disabled, can adultery be justified?

It's an issue that crops up in many a made-for-TV movie, but experts say it's largely a phony one.

Dorothy Smith, the director of nursing staff development at Houston's famed M.D. Anderson Cancer Center, deals with many seriously ill patients.

She estimates that **70 percent of all sexual problems brought about by illness can be overcome with open communication and loving intimacy.** "Cancer cannot destroy sexuality," she notes. "Their sexuality is part of the person."

There is more to sex than the standard form of genital intercourse. If there is love and commitment and caring— and a little inventiveness—means to make physical love can be found.

If one partner is filled with frustration, however, a discussion about wants and needs with the other is in order, providing the spouse can handle the conversation. If the two of you decide, after frank communication, that the healthy partner should seek sexual gratification elsewhere, that's no one's business but your own. Be prepared to renegotiate, though, if the situation changes. Keep lines of communication open, and remember: **If one partner thinks there's a problem, there's a problem.**

Often, a healthy spouse is needlessly afraid of hurting the ailing partner, especially if the latter has had a heart attack. In these cases, both of you should ask the cardiologist frankly when sexual relations can resume, and to what extent, and then discuss the situation together.

When Gene had his coronary at age forty-five, his wife, Dody, couldn't get over her terror that he would die. While the two remained emotionally close, she could not bring herself to make love to him, lest another attack occur. Since he had many of the same concerns, he was content to drift along platonically.

But then Dody had an affair. He found out, and in the course of counseling, they came to realize they both desperately missed their sexual connection, yet were afraid to bring up the subject.

Fear of dying sometimes motivates infidelity among patients, too. Perry, for example, was told by his oncologist that his cancer was terminal. He went out and had three affairs in rapid succession, trying to live it up while he still had time.

IMPOTENCE

Impotence affects about 10 million men. It is frequently mentioned as a justification for affairs, but that is less and less defensible. Increasingly, doctors have found that the disorder has correctable physical causes. Diabetes is the culprit in 2.5 million cases. Several common prescription drugs for high blood pressure, diabetes, and some allergies, for instance, can as a side effect cause impotence; substitute medications can be used.

In two of my cases, the solution was as simple as reducing or stopping the dosage of allergy medicine my patients were taking.

There are some promising chemical treatments as well as several varieties of penile prostheses available to enhance performance.

And if the causes are psychological, therapy may also be highly effective. Should the impotence be based on anxiety, the rediscovery of touching, stroking, and other forms of sexual pleasure not only can erase the problem but lead to a better sex life overall.

Having an affair may release your sexual frustrations—but it certainly won't help your mate's problem. Given all those good alternatives, shouldn't those who love each other try other remedies first?

SHOULD YOU TELL?

When people have achieved true intimacy without fear and feel safe with one another, I believe they do not desire outside relationships. There's no room or energy for more than one relationship that intense at a time!

It is difficult-to-impossible to be in two places at once.

But suppose you have *already* committed the so-called unforgivable sin?

Should you keep the transgression secret?

In most cases, no.

You do need to assess your own relationship. There are some circumstances in which disclosure could blow the relationship out of the water. If your partner is already suffering deeply—from the death of a parent or a child for example— and you do not believe he or she could handle the news at this time, you may want to postpone it.

Consider your motive. Don't tell just to make yourself feel better; this is something your partner will remember the rest of his life.

You must also be very careful about the manner in which you tell. Many seem almost eager to flaunt the details, which will only make the damage worse.

Lifting Shame and Guilt

In the next part of this book, I'm going to show you how to work through confession and anguish to a lasting, loving amnesty.

Before you can do that, however, you have to unburden yourselves of guilt and shame. Most adulterous husbands or wives will sooner or later develop a heavy heart. To lighten it, they need to share with the one they love best.

Unless they tell, they cannot take responsibility and cannot be forgiven.

Secrecy encourages the affair to continue, and **it is the resultant guilt, not lack of love, that breaks up many couples.**

In most cases, to be sure, the spouse already knows—or has decided to deny knowledge or even collude, as we've seen. And the children, as we've also seen, almost always know.

I am not as insistent on absolute honesty as some therapists, however. I believe that not telling is defensible in some cases, especially when the behavior was fleeting and is past history, and the participant is working to deal with the underlying causes.

Anyone who has had an affair and is uncertain about whether to tell, though, should certainly go for counseling. Many adulterous individuals consult me on their own, for example, wanting to end the illicit relationship but unsure when or how to do so.

How to Confess to an Affair

In two-thirds of the cases where the betrayal is known, the cheating partner will confess to his or her mate; in the rest, outsiders inform or clues lead the mate to this wrenching discovery.

However it happens, the disclosure is always explosive. But there are ways to minimize the damage:

FOR THE DECEIVER

1. Make sure when you tell that you are motivated by a real desire to improve the relationship, not merely to unload guilt or—worse—to gloat.

2. Do not confess in anger. Cool down and make an appointment for a later time. Say you have something important to discuss.

3. Timing is crucial. Consider your partner's level of self-esteem, other crises or pressures. Otherwise hold off and get professional help with this step.

4. Try to reassure your mate that he or she is loved. Mention good times that you two have shared. Validate what's said. Don't be defensive, blaming, or hostile.

5. Use talking techniques described in "Fighting" (page 122) and at the end of the next three chapters.

6. Keep talking, even if it takes many hours. Do *not* shut the other person out. At this point, he or she may feel on the verge of a nervous breakdown.

7. Be willing to answer questions about your lover...but not too explicitly. If you don't answer these questions, your partner will dwell on them, imagining the worst, and become obsessed.

Do not, however, defend your lover. Be prepared for attacks on that person, but don't get angry back.

8. Expect anger, shock, tears, recriminations. Do not expect immediate forgiveness, even if you apologize.

9. Many who have affairs have difficulty talking about their feelings—which is why they had affairs in the first place. *Don't retreat into silence.*

10. Be honest about whether you're going to end the affair. To establish credibility and mend the relationship, you have to stop.

FOR THE DECEIVED

How to ask:

1. Confront your mate with your suspicions even if you're afraid of the answers and afraid he or she will leave. Otherwise, you give tacit permission for the affair to continue. State firmly: "I think you are having an affair." Do not ask open-ended questions.

2. Be assertive but not judgmental.

3. Be direct. Don't hint or beat around the bush.

4. Don't send dual messages, saying "If you are, I don't want to know," or "If I ever find out, I'll leave."

5. Face the betrayer and look him/her in the eye. Do not permit diversions such as television. Do not drink before, during, or after.

6. If your partner changes the subject, state it again and stick to the subject only.

7. Your partner may say you're crazy, blame you, storm out, accuse you of having an affair yourself. Don't let this reaction rattle you and return to the subject as soon as you can. Validate, keep a poker face, and don't shoot back.

8. Understand that your mate is also going through hell, compounded by guilt, rage, sorrow, and shame. There is real pain on his/her side, too. Try to be supportive of that.

The more you can reduce the guilt that torments your partner, the less likely he/she will bolt.

9. Don't ever say, "It's all my fault." *Don't ever make excuses.*

10. State the consequences if the affair continues. Demand that it end.

FOR BOTH

Once it is out in the open, you should seek counseling or family therapy to help determine the whys of the affair, so that it doesn't happen again. **If you're separated don't go back without first seeking help or taking a stand about the affair.**

For tips on channeling the anger that arises, see the heading in the following chapter, "For the Betrayed."

THE BEGINNINGS OF FORGIVENESS

Now that we better understand the sin, let's begin striving for forgiveness.

The process is enormously demanding. **If you are the betrayed,** you must understand how difficult it is for your partner to give up this undemanding, satisfying, thrilling relationship. Remember, it is often rooted in childhood pain. You won't want to hear that, but you must. On the other hand, you should not resume the relationship without genuine signs of commitment to change.

If you are the betrayer, you must comprehend the damage you've done, and be willing to wrestle with the emotional wounds that led you to do it. You must put forth all that effort, meanwhile, without the satisfaction and support of your paramour.

So before you begin, ask yourself these questions:

Quiz: Are You Ready to Forgive?

In the following chapters, I'll show you how to vent your anger, admit your grief, and find real-life love. But first, you may want to ask yourself whether you think that goal is worth struggling for.

FOR BOTH PARTNERS

1. Do I think my marriage or relationship is worth saving?
2. Am I willing to set and uphold guidelines for fidelity?
3. Am I willing to question my parents about whether this is a family pattern? To tell them about the emptiness inside of me?
4. Am I willing to work together to ease our children's anxieties?
5. Am I still sexually interested in my partner? Most importantly, do I still love him or her? Does he/she still love me?
6. Am I forgiving and is the family I grew up in forgiving?

FOR THE BETRAYED

1. Did I contribute in any way to the distance between us and am I willing to change my behavior?
2. Do I feel anything but fury or hatred when I look at my partner? If I learn how, can I give up my grudges and forget my obsession with the other lover?
3. Have I given my mate an ultimatum and a deadline for ending the affair?
4. Am I willing to trust and be vulnerable again, even if it means getting hurt?

FOR THE BETRAYER

1. Am I willing to give up the affair?
2. Am I willing to delve into the pain and emptiness inside myself to explore my real reasons for doing this, including meeting with my parents?
3. Am I willing to listen to criticism? Even when it's harsh and hurtful?
4. Am I willing to devote the time and effort to change and commit to this relationship?

Give yourself 2 points for every positive reply. If your total is 8 or more, you're on the threshold of forgiveness.

· 9 ·

Go Ahead, Get Angry!

So now you know the terrible truth.
What do you do?

Susan Suffers in Silence

If you're like long-suffering Susan—and a surprising number of us are—you try to ignore your anguish, in hopes it will go away.

The day Susan discovered that her husband, Lyle, was cheating, she actually went so far as to cook his favorite meal, pot roast, for dinner. A friend of her mother's had tattled that Lyle was carrying on with a local boutique-owner. Susan was hurt, humiliated, and angry, but she never said a word. "I didn't want to be a bitch," she later explained in her soft-spoken way.

Lyle knew that she knew, however—her mother had informed him of the fact. Knotted with guilt, he waited and waited for the attack that never came. "She is absolutely driving me crazy with her niceness," he sighed.

In truth, Susan nearly drove *herself* crazy. She was referred to me by her family doctor because she was experiencing depression and suicidal feelings.

Anger is a corrosive emotion. If you bottle it up inside, it will eat away at your self-respect—and it will come out anyway, sooner or later, in some destructive way.

But Susan and Lyle, two adult children of adulterers, were too terrified to admit what they were feeling. Only after months of therapy did these overly polite people begin to acknowledge their emptiness and resentment.

Lyle's parents had maintained a mannerly but frozen marriage with no fighting. Now, after thirty years, they were getting a divorce. He was incensed at his unfaithful dad.

Susan had always tried to pump up her low self-esteem by being the nicest person around. She tried to hide, even from herself, the fact that she was just as furious now over her husband's infidelity as she had always been about her father's.

Using exercises found at the end of this chapter, the couple finally unleashed their furies and defanged them. "I can't trust you, you're just like my father!" Susan screamed—the first time she had ever raised her voice to Lyle. "My lover always tells me how she feels," he shot back. "She does not 'betray me with polite lies.'"

This was healthy progress. Lyle wanted and needed limits. They made him realize how much his wife cared. We had sessions with their parents, too. This couple *was* willing to do the necessary work to exorcise childhood demons as well as get the marriage running again. They all became allies, and proceeded to the next step—mourning and forgiveness—which you'll read about in the following two chapters.

FEAR OF FURY

It is only natural to be outraged by adultery. It is, after incest, the strictest sexual taboo in our society and strikes right to the very soul of trust.

But society also trains us to minimize conflict, and most of us fear our own hostility to some extent. Do any of these feelings sound familiar?

- You are afraid of being abandoned, so you think you should settle for peace at any price.
- You have been taught to feel sorry for a sinner.
- You feel you are overreacting...maybe everybody *is* doing it.
- Nice people/ladies/grown-ups don't get angry.
- If you don't talk about it, it will go away.
- Once you lose control, the next step could be mayhem or murder.

When she swallowed her anger, Susan was following a typical female pattern. I have observed that women are likelier than men to suffer diminished self-esteem in these circumstances. "Of course, he left me for that beautiful young girl," a middle-aged woman may rationalize.

What's more, women frequently get repressive advice from friends or well-meaning clergymen who believe in turning the other cheek. "Don't worry, it doesn't mean anything. You have children to think about," they soothe.

Wrong. Even if you do think most men do it, adultery is not acceptable. *There is no room for another person between two people who want to be close. Remember:* **A triangle can become a wedge.**

It's been my experience that men, on the other hand, have less trouble venting their anger. *A man who finds out that his wife is having an affair tends to take immediate action.* He'll go right to the phone and tell the guy to back off, or he'll confront the lovers directly, even violently.

Sometimes, the confrontations are dramatic.

Chad and Millicent both had keys to their friend Nate's downtown Manhattan apartment, which they used when they wanted to shower and change for an evening out without returning to their home in the suburbs.

Then Chad learned Millicent was using the place for

something else—and with Nate. Finding out by eavesdropping on an extension when the couple's next tryst was to be, Chad arranged a memorable welcome. He not only "frenched," or shortsheeted the bed, he rigged up a tar bucket over the front door. Millicent came home with bits of tar still stuck in her hair—and no possibility of denying her involvement!

Often, men lose control....

John, a lawyer whose wife, Sally, was vice president of a large insurance firm, came home early from a business trip to find his wife cozily entwined on their bed with her boss, Scott, watching porno movies. Everyone started screaming. Since he could scarcely excuse himself or Sally, Scott went on the attack. "If you'd been taking care of her better, we wouldn't be here in the first place!" he taunted.

That remark so incensed John that he punched Scott, and Sally's paramour, four inches shorter and thirty pounds lighter than her husband, was knocked out cold, with blood flowing from his nose.

But John wasn't finished with his revenge. First he called Scott's wife, Michelle, to inform her...and to suggest she tell their kids. Then he called in his own children, ages four and seven, to tell them that their mother was acting like "a whore." This charge frightened the little boy, even though he wasn't quite sure what it meant. "Daddy, are we getting a new mommy because of what Mommy did?" John, Jr., asked in a quavering voice.

Even in these dire circumstances, it was possible to salvage the relationship, but only because both parties were determined.

Sally, it turned out, resented John's domineering ways and feared his violent temper. She'd never been able to stand up to him successfully, however. This affair was her last-ditch attempt to either stabilize her marriage or be forced to leave it, once and for all.

After Scott fired her in retaliation for what John had done

to his own family, Sally realized Scott was not the man she wanted, either. Then, when John declared he was going to leave, she realized she still loved him.

She didn't realize for quite some time, though, that she was reenacting an old family script. Only in multigenerational therapy did it emerge that Sally's mother, Wanda—controlling, just like John—had been an adulteress. Sally, she finally blurted out, was the illegitimate offspring of her affair with a married man. Her strictness was partly due to her shame. (The family legacy had reached all three of Wanda's children: Sally and her brother both cheated, while her sister married a man who was unfaithful.)

John, meanwhile, eventually faced his own resentment of a domineering mother and his vindictive rage at Sally—as well as the chronic drinking that fueled both. Remarkably, not only he and Sally, but Scott and Michelle—who also came in, separately, of course—were able to channel their anger effectively and make their marriages survive.

Here are five steps to help do the same with your feelings, followed by exercises to get you through this stage and on to the next. To help you recall them, their first letters spell **ANGER.**

ADMIT you're angry. Go ahead! Give yourself permission to be outraged. Don't feel guilty or apologetic. You have a right to feel this way. Adultery administers a huge insult to you and your relationship. It has gotten more than one murderer off on grounds of justifiable homicide.

And if you don't acknowledge these feelings, they will burn forever inside you. Hurt lies below the anger, and love is underneath the hurt, but you can't get these without going through this first.

NEGATE your negative urges. Don't retaliate by having an affair yourself or try to numb the pain by drinking, eating, or getting yourself fired. Take one day at a time.

GIVE vent to your feelings—harmlessly.

- **Take a long walk to a secluded spot where you can shout; scream into a pillow in a closed room;**

- punch a punching bag or pillow;
- take a furiously fast walk, run, or swim;
- stomp steps in an aerobics class, on a stair machine, or do the real thing;
- call up a good friend or relative who will listen without advising or badmouthing your spouse.

EVALUATE any contribution you may have made to the affair. Did you set limits and enforce them? Did you make your needs known? Did you create a triangle of your own—with the kids or your job—to distance your mate? Without recognizing these errors, you can't change and move on.

REMEMBER the love you two once had for each other. Trying to renew it will help you survive the pain and reach reconciliation.

Following are some patient-tested exercises to help you acknowledge your feelings and reach your next goal. These exercises have been adapted especially for adultery from marital-conflict exercises designed by Dr. Harville Hendrix and by Lori Gordon, M.S.W., founder of PAIRS (Practical Application to Intimate Relationship Skills).

To make these exercises succeed, **both** partners must pledge to devote time and energy to them.

Exercise One: Expressing Your Anger

As we've seen, anger is a poisonous emotion. You must handle it with care. Hold it in, and it can destroy you; let it explode, and it can destroy everyone else you care about. Follow these steps to detoxify your anger before you vent it on your partner.

1. *Write letters. Deposit daily in what one of my professors, Dr. Phillip Guerin of the Center for Family Learning, calls a "Bitter Bank."*

You should come up with one of these a day and put it in a folder for your eyes only. Do not—repeat, do NOT—mail it or show it to anyone.

Letter No. 1: Write only "I hate you, (spouse's name)," as many times as you can—ideally, more than seventy times.

Letter No. 2: Tell your mate how hurt, angry, and sad you are about what happened, how much you hate him/her in response, and how you want to leave. Ask why he/she betrayed you.

Letter No. 3: Explain how much you love and need your partner and why you can't let go. Describe your fear of abandonment and what life would be like without your mate.

Letter No. 4: Compose the letter you wish your spouse would send in response. Put in everything you want to hear— apology, rationale, regrets, and penance for the adultery, nice things your partner is going to do to try and make it up to you, what a wonderful, loving person you are (and how much you are loved and missed). Have your spouse beg you not to leave and grovel about how unworthy he/she is; tell you how sorry he/she is to abuse you after all the wonderful things you've done; describe how he/she will ask for forgiveness and recommit to you and your marriage from now on.

Letter No. 5: Mark down any part you may have played in all of this. Address it to your partner, and this time—deliver it. Equalizing the responsibility reduces your anger, obsession, and feelings of victimization. Here, *you* ask for forgiveness.

Letters No. 6-10: Repeat all the previous letters, but this time address them to the parent that you are most distant from or who hurt you most with some kind of betrayal—if not adultery, then by being cold, demanding, selfish, neglectful, or by never being there.

Letters No. 11–15: Repeat all previous letters but this time address them to your other parent.

Read your parental letters to your partner. Help him or her understand the relationship of today's hurts to yesterday's. This will dissipate some anger.

You must deposit your letters daily in your file or "bitter bank" for one week to three months, until you feel your anger diminish. Try not to dwell on your anger, however, except in the time set aside every day for banking your bitterness.

It's healthy to be bitter, but it's unhealthy to stay stuck at that stage. You have to gradually work through your anger to the hurt to reach the love and forgiveness. This is not easy. At first, you *will* be obsessed by thoughts of the lover, and you will nurse your bitterness. You may not be able to sleep, or you may sleep too much. You may be unable to eat, or you may want to stuff yourself. You may have difficulty concentrating.

By working with these feelings, though, you will come to control them, rather than being possessed by them.

If you find yourself unable to get beyond this stage, however, seek professional help. Make sure to find a therapist who will counsel both of you—together and possibly separately—as well as your children.

If you are successful with your Bitter Bank, advance to:

2. *Deconstruct your triangle.*

You cannot communicate with your betrayer until there is an equal sign between you and responsibility is shared. If you continue to play the roles of victim-saint and scoundrel, you will not hear or heal each other. You will probably end up divorcing without having solved your problems.

Draw a triangle and write the name of each person involved at each of the points.

Do the same for your family of origin.

Note your problems in a few sentences underneath each triangle. Note similarities.

SAMPLE: I could not accept his workaholism. It reminded me of my father's rejections as a kid, so I had an affair.

List your contributions to the problem. Ask other people (family and friends) who know you both for their opinions. How did that person get into the triangle? Do you keep people at a certain emotional distance because of your own fears of intimacy and inability to trust? Did you put other people and things first?

For each of your own contributions to the problem, **list** at least one and preferably two or three ways to change your behavior and help the cause.

Next to each alternative, **write out** the changes in behavior you hope these adjustments will inspire in your partner.

SAMPLE: If I learn to play golf and keep him company, he won't spend so much time hanging out at the country club without me. We might share more, and he would give up the affair. Then **evaluate** the cost or benefit to you of these changes (yours and theirs). Explain that while learning golf and joining him might leave you with less free time for yourself, you'll have more fun and intimacy together. Maybe the trade-off is well worth it.

Consider whether or not you are being a runaway. If so you would have to own why you have been distancing as well.

Exercise Two: Confrontation

Once you have a better grasp of your feelings, you are ready to make them known to your mate.

Expect turmoil, tears, scenes—these are powerful emotions you are attempting to channel.

A few ground rules may help.

FOR THE BETRAYED

1. Don't call a divorce lawyer!

2. Do understand that most runaways (the predominant strain of adulterers) are allergic to emotionality. Provide frequent time-outs; try not to overload your mate's system.

3. Insist the affair end; otherwise, no change can occur.

4. Take your share of responsibility but do not shoulder all of the blame.

5. Don't try to forgive before you grapple with your anger, hurt, and pain.

6. Tell the truth—don't minimize your anguish.

7. Reach out—reconnect with parents, siblings, friends. As a pursuer, **you are likely to feel isolated, and it is crucial**

for you to take your loneliness back to the family you grew up in and deal with the betrayal.
8. Promise yourself you will try to get beyond bitterness.
9. Try not to lose control of yourself.
10. Take a stand. Risk abandonment—you're abandoned anyway.

FOR THE BETRAYER

You may hate this emotional situation, but the more you distance, the wilder it will make your partner. Call for a time out when you need breathing space.
1. Deal with facts, not fantasies. Try to see the lover for what he or she really is, flaws and all.
2. Don't blame the victim, whose self-esteem is already suffering. Don't displace your guilt onto your mate.
3. Recognize you can't and won't—and shouldn't—be forgiven immediately, no matter how many times you apologize.
4. Don't squelch, deny, ignore, or minimize the feelings of your mate. Expect darts to be thrown, and don't get angry back.
5. Be patient and validate your partner.
6. Take responsibility for your actions.
7. Realize that your hardest task is to regain your partner's trust. Giving up the affair is a first step.
8. Keep talking, talking, talking. Be prepared for yelling, threats of divorce, even having objects thrown at you. Your partner will be provocative as well as critical. Your commitment is being tested.
Now you may begin the exercises.

THE BULLETPROOF VEST EXERCISE

Step 1: Complaint

Request an appointment to talk with your mate. Be honest about the topic: You will be venting your pain and anger over this betrayal.

Set a specific time limit to make the prospect less forbidding: say, twenty minutes per person. Request and honor time-outs if the discussion becomes too intense.

Set a deadline for an RSVP; you must have a response within twenty-four hours. Do not ignore this deadline.

Make it clear that you know you may not wind up staying together; you are simply trying to deal with the pain you feel and determine if there is any hope for the relationship.

Tell your spouse to come prepared with a figurative "bulletproof vest" and be prepared to take the darts, slings, arrows, and low blows that are going to fly.

Your spouse has to promise not to be defensive, to hear and validate your complaints, and to resist the impulse to reply. You will both have your turns. You must also pledge not to use what is said during these free-speaking sessions against each other later.

Avoid distractions. No television, no reading or knitting, no alcohol before, during, or after.

If the spouse accepts the appointment, he or she must sit attentively, "wearing" their vest and absorbing the pain, the anger and hurt.

Try to see your partner as a wounded child. When it's your turn, keep going until you reach deep into your childhood. Are you, like Debbi, terrified of being abandoned because that once happened to you when you were little?

The purpose of this exercise is to validate the normal feelings of rage induced by betrayal. It is to get behind that anger to the hurt and the yearning for love.

Let your partner vent and listen. Even when you don't agree, don't argue; simply sympathize with the honest hurt.

If the deceiver refuses to participate in these exercises, saying something like, "I don't want to hear about it," get professional help immediately. You cannot do this on your own.

Step 2: Echo

The adulterer proves he/she was listening by playing back the statements of the betrayed. The betrayed then notes if anything was skipped over or misinterpreted, and in this case, the adulterer tries again.

We are all self-centered; when someone else talks, we only listen partially. These are important listening skills to learn. **The echo exercise is essential in reconstructing a relationship.**

Don't get discouraged if it takes a long time to do this. The alleged listener needs to repeat as many times as it takes before the message is received. Whether or not there is agreement is not the point.

Echo without intruding. For example, if the victimized mate says, "I feel you don't love me because you had an affair with so and so," simply repeat that: "You feel I don't love you because I had an affair with so and so."

Resist the impulse to interject: "I had an affair because *you* ignored me."

Step 3: Validation

Acknowledge that you understand these are your spouse's true feelings and that he/she has a right to them. Validation is not about agreement.

Example: "I can see how unloved you must feel because I had the affair."

Again, this does not mean it's time to get defensive. Don't slip in a countercharge here by adding, "But if you hadn't been so consumed by your goddamn job, I wouldn't have done it." This type of response is self-centered and blocks progress.

Feelings are not true or false or right or wrong. You are expected to put yourself in your partner's shoes and "hear where they're coming from." Without validation, you can't go on to mutual understanding, exchanging confidences, and achieving intimacy.

Step 4: Empathize

If you can understand your mate's feelings, you'll have more of a chance of achieving intimacy. You can't have closeness without empathy. *Example*: "I can see how hurt and angry you feel." Check out the feeling with your partner to see if you have empathized correctly. If not, echo your partner's feelings.

In my practice I often see that *it is not the actual affair that drives couples to divorce but the inability or unwillingness of one spouse to understand what the other is going through. This is the inability to validate and empathize.*

If you can do this part of the exercise, even if it takes a year, you can eventually achieve forgiveness and a stronger relationship.

Step 5: Reversal

Switch vests and roles and do the exercises above again.

Now it's time for the deceiver to rise to his or her own defense. You can attack back, justify your actions, make accusations. You can talk about how distressed you are to give up the affair. You can criticize your mate's failings and reveal all the hurts and inattentiveness you suffered that led you to stray.

Talk about how you feel displaced by the new baby...terrified of turning forty...scared you'll be laid off. Tell how you are hurting inside and why you chose to fill up your emptiness with an affair. You can declare that you really wish you could go back to the romantic days.

And this time, the deceived has to sit there quietly and take it all in. There's a natural instinct to bridle, to say, "Wait a second...how dare you...*I'm* the injured party here." But wearing his or her bulletproof vest, the mate needs to listen to the cheater's own pain. Remember:

PEOPLE WHO ARE NOT IN SOME SORT OF PAIN DO NOT COMMIT ADULTERY.

THE EMBRACEABLE YOU EXERCISE

The above exercises strip away layer after layer of pretense, to reveal the naked, wounded child within. They can be done with partners or, as we'll see later, with parents.

One at a time, after each person has vented his feelings as above, the listener must cradle and soothe this aching soul. Try to rock and hold the person for fifteen minutes. Cry together. Talk about childhood hurts that influenced your grown-up behavior and about the pain that still haunts you.

If you are the betrayed, something magical may happen. You may stop seeing your mate as your enemy, the villain, and see the lonely, aching child this person used to be. **Embracing that child doesn't mean you excuse the adulterer's behavior; it does mean you hear the cry for help.**

If you are the betrayer, you may be able to see how your mate was suffering long before meeting you. That may help you to reduce your anger and guilt and encourage you to sympathize.

My mother and I had abandoned my father for his scandalous behavior, for example, until that magical moment in Dr. Fogarty's office when we finally perceived him as a scared, hurt ten-year-old boy who had lost his way. I had been very angry, but I felt my feelings melt into tenderness. He, in turn, began to look at his mother, his wife, and his daughter differently. Only then did we begin the long, hard journey to forgiveness.

This exercise is essential because it is only when we work out our issues with our parents that we are able to love others truly.

BEHAVIOR WISH LISTS

As each partner emerges from this comforting embrace, he/she should list three changes in behavior that could help ease the heartaches. The more changes each of you lists the better it will be for the relationship. Keep in mind that what you want the most from your partner will be the hardest for them to give.

The listener *must* agree to at least one and up to three—if it is absolutely certain he/she will deliver.

EXAMPLES:

- I want you to spend more time with me.

- I want you to come home from the office before 8:00 P.M. because it makes me trust you more.
- I want you to stop mentioning your lover.

These changes are *not* easy, but by changing to please your partner, you will become less selfish and more giving.

PENANCE

In almost all cases, the betrayed is so exceptionally angry or obsessed by the affair that the betrayer must prove his good faith (and suffer) before they can proceed, and the betrayed can see their part. In these situations, both need to agree upon a "penance" to be extracted within a specific period of time. (This doesn't go on forever!)

One of my patients punished her philandering spouse by splurging madly on her credit cards for 8 hours—as agreed beforehand. Her husband picked up the $5,000 tab. As it should be, the penance was discussed, agreed upon, and accomplished in a limited amount of time.

Exercise Three: Fighting

Sometimes, after discovering adultery, you just want to give someone hell. When the hostility gets to be too much, try these time-limited exercises for catharsis adapted from PAIRS (Practical Application of Intimate Relationship Skills) and George Bach's book *The Intimate Enemy.*

Ranting, raving, screaming, insults, accusations, crying, and cursing—anything short of physical blows—are all allowed. As always, you must ask permission, make an appointment, and limit the time.

THE ONE-MINUTE DONNYBROOK

This time, don't listen to each other. Yell and scream and talk at the same time—it will probably sound a lot like your old arguments. Holler everything you ever thought about this person when you heard about the affair, plus all the resentments you've acquired over the years.

The catch is, you only have a minute. Use your oven timer—and heed it.

THE SIXTEEN-MINUTE WAR

Make an appointment for this ritualized battle. Each wears ear plugs or a walkman and uses the timer. Flip a coin to see who goes first.

Each has two four-minute intervals to rage. The other one doesn't have to listen, though. Encourage yourself to be as intense as you can.

MONOLOGUE

Each of you gets to deliver a five-to-fifteen minute diatribe, while the other doesn't speak. No lashing back allowed, but you must listen. No validation or behavior change is required.

LASH THE LOVER (TIME-LIMITED BY PERMISSION OF THE ADULTERER)

The betrayed gets to attack the Other Object of Affections, ask questions, and complain about how this has ruined his/her life. This is the ONLY time this can be done, although you can go through the exercise as often as needed provided you stop when the adulterer has had enough. The betrayer cannot respond, defend, or protect the lover as they usually do, except to answer questions. (As I've noted, this exercise will help relieve the betrayed's anger and fend off obsession. The more you tell, the less they dwell.) **Warning: If you don't play by the rules, you could send your partner back to the lover.**

Caution: Some questions are better left unvoiced or at least unanswered. Do you really want a graphic description of where and when and how the sex was done? Do you think you will ever be able to erase that picture from your mind?

Don't ever say to the betrayed, "I never loved you, anyway."

If the deceived mate does ask, the deceiver should resist the impulse to seek revenge by boastfulness—unless he/she doesn't care about ever putting things back together again.

Resist, too, the common impulse to defend your inamorata by saying, "She's prettier—and better in bed!" even if the accusations are unfair or untrue. If you do, you may destroy the foundation of your relationship beyond repair.

For the Adulterer, Some Legitimate Questions to Expect:
- Who?
- Where—on marital turf?
- How long has this been going on?
- When did you meet?
- Will you stop?
- Do you love this person?
- Will you leave and marry this person?
- Who else knows?
- Do you still love me?

Lighten Up

The preceding exercises can be exhausting and emotionally searing. After you do them, you should always relieve the tensions with some playfulness, which is just what many adulterous marriages lack.

You can also try one of these techniques whenever you feel the need to let off steam. They encourage your laughter. You should exaggerate it, huffing a hearty ho-ho-ho! At least thirty seconds of full-bodied laughter releases endorphins, the body's own feel-good chemicals—and you could use some right now.

PILLOW FIGHTING

The Japanese call this *Shindai,* or bed fighting. Couples often practice it when angry, believing the excitement of the battle stimulates passion and leads to making love. Some hotels even provide special rooms with extra pillows just for this exercise.

Take two old feather pillows and make a small slit in each so the feathers can really fly—literally. Have a set time; plan your strategy!

Then hit each other. You might start by venting any leftover anger, but eventually you'll most likely be laughing. The physical exercise, the anger release, the play, and the belly laughs are all healing.

If the betrayer runs out of feathers first, he/she must kneel down, touch each of the opponent's toes, and make a "humble apology" (for the affair) before assuming the fetal position so the victor can finish off the loser.

If the betrayed is the loser and wishes to withdraw from the fight, he/she can throw down the pillow and declare, "I give in and stroke you." This partner then does so, starting with the other's pillow, before moving toward the partner behind it. He/she also apologizes for any contribution to the affair and assumes the position of total humility.

Other exercises to instill what Dr. Hendrix calls "relaxed joyfulness":

MERRY-GO-ROUND

To stimulate a sense of play that's usually missing, take each other's hands and whirl around the room until you break into hearty laughter of thirty seconds or more. Look each other in the eyes and finish with a hug.

HIGH JUMP

See who can jump higher and end with a hearty laugh, as above.

CHIMPANZEE

Make like a monkey, jabbering and scratching, and make each other laugh.

Remember the two foolproof laughter provokers, if all else fails: Tickle each other; or have one partner put his head on the stomach of the partner who *is* able to laugh...it's contagious!

• 10 •

Not for Lovers Only

W hat makes someone become the Other Woman or Other Man in an adulterous triangle?

The same hidden motivations that send married people into the arms of another apply to lovers as well: unmet early needs, unacknowledged since childhood. Like all of us, they fear abandonment. Often, they also fear being engulfed and smothered by a demanding partner: If they pick someone married, they lessen that threat.

A married paramour also permits the lover to rebuild the Oedipal triangle from his or her youth—only this time, they get to romance their opposite-sex parent!

In many cases, lovers have low self-esteem. They feel they don't really deserve more than this part-time involvement. True, the arrangement has its compensations. The lover gets to see her swain or his sweetheart at their ardent best, and never has to suffer with them through income taxes.

But eventually, the half loaf turns out to be sour dough. **If the lover pushes for any degree of commitment, the affair, like all relationships, shifts from the honeymoon stage to the power struggle. And in 95 percent of the cases, this is a**

power struggle lovers cannot win. If they're going to have to devote effort to a relationship, the errant spouses reason, why not go back to the one where there's already a considerable investment?

Remember what the Nick Nolte character told the Barbra Streisand heroine in *Prince of Tides* when he left her to return to his wife? When she asked if he loved the wife more, he replied no, but he loved her longer.

Even if they do marry, these new mates will always glance nervously over their shoulders, concerned about repeating the pattern. With good reason: Both adultery and divorce rates run much higher in second marriages.

Thus lovers, too, often have good reason to rue their involvements with philanderers.

Following are some of their stories.

Daddy's Big Girl

Betty was a classic example of what happens to adored little girls like Crystal (from chapter 5) if boundaries are not set early on. A bubbly, attractive copywriter in her early thirties, Betty seemed almost proud of her Other Woman status. "I'm destined to be unhappy in love," she announced when she arrived in my office. "I've had three broken engagements, and I'm now involved with a married man for the third time."

Her father had treasured her as a child, then rejected her when she reached puberty. In therapy—and with great difficulty—she finally began to realize that her upbringing was confused and inconsistent. By picking married men again and again she was still competing with her glamorous mother for the love of her charming dad.

"My mother is a beauty," Betty confided. "Everyone thinks so. She's a big fashion executive. Of course, she spends a lot of time at the beauty parlor. She's always criticizing my hair and my clothes."

Betty had great problems with intimacy. Whenever someone began to draw near, whenever things were going well, she bolted because she felt guilty.

During our sessions, Betty found a married man who fell in love with her and divorced his wife. He wanted to marry Betty. Once again, she fled, losing interest, finding fault with him and then cheating, as she had always cheated before.

Before she came to see me for family-of-origin work, Betty had been in individual therapy for thirteen years. She was all too willing to blame her parents for her problems, but unwilling to deal with the emptiness that resulted. She could not, therefore, break free of this pattern by reconnecting with her mother and father. Every time we made progress, she would stop showing up for appointments. She finally fled from me as she had run from relationships. To this day, she is still going from one man to another.

I'll Fly Away

Sydney, whom you met in chapter 3, was determined not to repeat the promiscuous ways of her twin brother, Seth.

But what did she do? *She chose Aldo, someone a lot like Seth.* Her mother's death when she was a teenager had made her particularly fearful of abandonment, yet she was also afraid to become too involved with a man who might leave her the way Seth had left three wives.

Enter Aldo, the dashing, debonair airline pilot long married to the elegant Carla, mother of his five children. He was the European-born son of a philandering father, and he had himself had many mistresses before Sydney. Somehow, though, she convinced herself that this time true love would win out, and he would marry her.

As a therapist, I often try to help lovers through denial or false hope by bringing in the married person. In Sydney's case, Aldo agreed because he was becoming worried about the degree of her obsession with him.

. When he came in alone, I asked if he had any intention of

leaving Carla for Sydney. He admitted that Carla was quite demanding, and he had sought someone simpler and more pliable. Sydney, he said with a slight laugh, was perhaps too much that way. "Sydney's a very nice person, but we come from different worlds. We're not the same religion. My family is very cultured. Sydney's father is a laborer. Her apartment is too modest in taste for me. She doesn't like sports. No, we do not have that much in common. She is making me very upset by wanting me to leave my wife and children."

What's more, this time Carla had put her foot down: If he left her, she would take the children and move far away, where he would not see them.

"Why are you leading Sydney on? Why don't you let her go?" I asked.

"She can go anytime," he shrugged.

In her individual sessions, Sydney focused on how neglected she had felt when her father put his work first and his motherless children second. Her twin brother was the favorite, and she felt overshadowed by him, as well. "Am I always going to be second, never number one?" she said. Nevertheless, the handsome Aldo could always lure her back to fantasyland. "I'm not strong enough to leave him," she sighed.

Finally, they both came to my office together. She demanded: "Make up your mind once and for all. Are you going to divorce Carla and marry me, or are we going to break it off for good?"

"I am an honorable man," Aldo responded. "It is against my religion to divorce. Besides, I would feel too guilty about leaving my wife and children."

Sydney broke down in tears at his reply—but the chains, at last, were severed.

Sydney began seeing an eligible man. As frequently happens with runaways, Aldo pursued her again when he heard she was otherwise engaged. This time, however, she wouldn't play the game.

Carla, meanwhile, was not so fortunate. She had come in to see me for a few therapy sessions. I tried to help her find a job and become more independent of Aldo. But after Sydney ditched him, he demanded that Carla cease therapy, lest she leave him, too.

I hear that they are still unhappily married and he is still cheating.

Beating the Biological Clock

Lisa almost paid a huge price for her delusions about the unavailable Alan. For one thing, this junior high teacher was thirty-five and eager to have a child—something her involvement with her married principal postponed.

"Alan promised me that he would leave his wife and marry me," Lisa said in a joint session. "If I made such a promise, it was in a moment of passion," said Alan, shifting uncomfortably in his chair. "She should have known from the beginning that our relationship, though wonderful, would never get any further. I want to be free."

Indeed he did. Alan, who came from a long line of Romeos, was stepping out on Lisa, too, just as he was on his wife. She received incontrovertible evidence of this when she contracted a case of genital warts from her hyperactive lover.

I had to take a strong stand and insist that I would not work with her until she stopped sleeping with him and brought him into therapy. I was also concerned, of course, with the fact that he might be passing along this potentially serious STD to his wife or other partners.

After Alan admitted that he had no intention of marrying Lisa, he promised to inform his lovers of their possible infection.

Even after those disclosures, though, Lisa maintained for many more individual sessions that she still loved him. She was only able to break free by working with her family—both in and out of sessions—to heal the childhood wounds inflicted by her perfectionist mother and father.

Both parents expected her to get A's and to excel at everything. Her mother was overclose as well as overdemanding, and Lisa felt engulfed by her attentiveness. Alan gave her the space she needed. He was also an authority figure from whom she could win approval. Who better to stand in for her mother than a school principal?

Because she was willing to go back, explore her emptiness, and come to terms with her parents, Lisa was able to move on. She is now married to a faithful man and was expecting her first child at this writing.

Unsafe Sex

As I have noted, some of my single patients manage to convince themselves that sleeping with married lovers is safer in this age of AIDS. As Lisa's case demonstrates, that is absolutely wrong.

Consider the sad case of Ann, a successful twenty-five-year-old model who was looking forward to her wedding. Years before her engagement, she had had a fling with a married man at a convention—and contracted herpes. She did not want to have sex with her fiancé without telling him, and brought him into therapy to make her disclosure in a neutral environment. He was too shocked and repulsed by the relevation to continue even with therapy, however, and eventually broke off the relationship.

The Ultimate Triangle

You don't have to be married to be an unfaithful, unavailable partner.

Just ask Shari or Elise, who were trapped in what might be the ultimate triangle with Tyrone, a handsome actor.

Shari, a twenty-eight-year-old TV producer, was deliriously happy when Tyrone proposed marriage. Then he went off on a trip without telling her. Worried when she didn't hear from him for a week, Shari let herself into his apartment with her key.

Inside, she pressed the automatic redial button on his phone.

A woman answered. "Who are you?"

"Who are *you*?" Elise replied.

"*I'm* Tyrone's girlfriend."

"No," said Shari, "that can't be, because *I'm* his fiancée."

"Well, *that* can't be," exploded Elise, "because *we* just got back from a week in Spain."

"But he proposed to *me!*" wailed Shari.

"Let's get together and talk," said a grim Elise.

They met, and exchanged some hurtful information. "You can have him after he lied!" said Shari. "I don't want him either," said Elise, an actress who had met Tyrone on location and had been dating him—exclusively, she thought—for nine months. "He thought he could get away with this."

The two decided to confront their wandering boy together, and were seated on his couch when he arrived home. "How could you do this to me?" Shari screamed. "You've got to choose," said Elise.

He said he was in love with both of them.

"Impossible," said Elise, insisting, "Now or never—choose!"

"He doesn't have to—I don't want him," said Shari, slamming out the door.

Elise and Tyrone stayed together for three weeks before he said he wanted to see Shari.

They took up their relationship, but without sex. Shari, who was my patient, said she kept visualizing him with Elise and felt repulsed. Still, she could not bring herself to leave permanently. She lost ten pounds she didn't want to lose, and she was miserable.

Tyrone came to see me. Now neither woman would make love to him, and he looked awful. He said he was genuinely heartbroken and confused. He was sickened by his inability to decide.

Months later, Shari concluded that if Tyrone did care enough for her, he would never have taken up with another. She broke off the relationship.

Eventually, Tyrone made a final break with Elise and returned to Shari. "He is all yours," Elise said after the break. "I know he really loves you and used me to get out of the commitment to marry you."

Not surprisingly, the wedding plans were put on hold. For now, Tyrone and Shari are proceeding very carefully, trying to deal with their mutual fear of intimacy first.

Thirty Ways to Leave Your Lover (With apologies to Paul Simon)

If you are a lover, you deserve something more. You can find it, as Lisa did, if you stop looking in the wrong places and look in the right ones.

1. Start with yourself. Own up to the fact that you are more comfortable with an unavailable lover. Admit your fear of intimacy and explore its roots.

2. Look back to the patterns of intimacy in your family. Track them on a genogram (see chapter 3).

3. Does illicit love or divorce run in your family?

4. Those who have trouble maintaining intimacy are probably not very close to their families—even though superficially, the opposite may be true. You may spend time with your family, but not really communicate with one or both your parents. Or you may keep them out of sight, but not out of mind.

Ask yourself how close you are to your parents and what resentments you may still be nursing.

5. Move toward forgiving the parent from whom you are most distant. If you keep having affairs with unavailable partners, there's almost certainly some form of betrayal in your past. Do the exercises in the following chapter on mourning.

6. If your estranged parent is dead, write him/her two letters—one for all the positive things you remember, the other for the negative side. Visit the grave and discuss both letters—silently, if you are too inhibited to read them aloud. Ask for more information about this parent from other relatives, so you can fill in their portrait and correct your child's-eye view.

Let Go

7. Don't torture yourself or your ex. Don't send sappy cards or make hang-up phone calls.

8. Stay away from the places you used to frequent.

9. Don't call up mutual friends and check up on how he or she is.

10. Don't use special events—a birthday, raise, promotion—as an excuse to rekindle the affair.

11. Ditto for sad occasions such as a death in the family. "But he *needs* me now," is destructive reasoning.

12. Get rid of clothing and mementos. Return what's his when you break up, mail it back, or burn or bury it.

13. If you work together, see if you can transfer to another department or even find a job elsewhere.

14. Let friends know you're available for fix-ups.

15. Don't drone on endlessly about the details of the relationship and the breakup. Even friends can get tired of it. Get angry, get sad—but get over it.

16. Resist the impulse to make yourself appear pitiful— eventually, you'll be embarrassed by it.

17. Learn your part in the triangle. How did it appeal to your deep-seated fears and needs?

18. Stop comparing every date or potential date to your ex; nobody can measure up to a myth.

19. Imagine your lover twenty years older and fifty pounds heavier.

20. Make a list of the lover's negative traits.

21. Get into circulation. Go to parties and meetings and seminars. You *don't* have to wait until you're entirely recovered from your anger and grief.

22. At a party, deliberately pick someone to talk to who's *not* your usual type. Maybe he/she isn't as perfectly dressed or coiffed, but your usual types haven't turned out so well.

And stay away from married people...you *know* that doesn't work! Make that a rule!

23. Go out with people who may seem boring or not terribly attractive at first glance. Again, your judgment has not always been perfect. And, as they say about the New York State lottery, Hey, you never know! Several of my single patients have ended up married to those they rejected at first.

Pickiness can sometimes mask fear.

24. Go on a vacation that will force you to meet and mingle.

25. Find new single friends of both sexes.

26. Find a project you really care about: volunteer work, taking night classes, writing a novel. Throw yourself into it during your spare time.

27. Repeatedly tell yourself you are willing to take risks again. Yes, you may get hurt, but hurt is a part of love.

28. Do give yourself time and opportunity to grieve for the lost relationship...but privately.

29. Change something noticeable about yourself that will boost your confidence. Streak your hair, lose ten pounds, get contacts, grow a beard or mustache, or get your teeth redone.

30. Take care of yourself. Eat right, exercise, don't beat up on yourself too much.

You deserve more than half a loaf.

Here are some exercises to help you through:

THE HOMELY LOVER

Three times a day, think negative thoughts about your lover. Imagine him/her fatter, older, sitting around in dirty pajamas.

Three times a day, visualize the adulterer with his/her own family. Think about what he/she is doing with spouse and children.

Visualize the family gathered around the Christmas tree. Feel how much they all miss him/her when not there.

SO LONG, SWEETHEART

Tap someone to stand in for your lover in this symbolic farewell—a friend or a parent. The parent you've been angry at, distant from, or betrayed by is ideal, if at all possible.

Then recall and renounce the memories of your affair. First, to make sure you're ready, the stand-in says, "What was it like being in the relationship together?" You reply. If you have nothing but wonderful memories to contribute, the stand-in asks for the negatives.

Then you "send off" the good times. Say, "I bid farewell to all the candlelit dinners, the flowers, the backrubs. I will never have them again."

Next, bid goodbye to all the terrible times as well. Stress the negatives, how you were an afterthought to the wife and children, how you never got weekends or holiday time.

Your stand-in should repeat and validate what you've said, expressing sympathy for your pain.

Have tissues ready. Let the parent or friend hold you, while you connect to childhood memories, the good and bad, looking for new ties while you sever old ones.

Finally, say farewell to your lover and the experiences of yesteryear...for good. Proclaim yourself free of your past and ready to move on...without looking back.

• 11 •

Grieving and Goodbyes

When adultery shatters their relationship, both partners lose something.

The betrayed feels as if she or he will never be able to trust or love wholeheartedly again. The betrayer feels he or she will never again find such flawless, undemanding love.

Both sides must mourn these losses before they can change and move on. Like any grief, the sorrow for a dead relationship goes through stages: denial, anger, guilt, acceptance. All stages must be experienced before couples can find forgiveness and rebirth. The process requires great courage, determination, and stamina—but the reward is lasting Real-Life Love.

You cannot ignore or obliterate these feelings.

Tom tried to do both when Gina ran away with another man after just one year of marriage. His pent-up emotions caused him terrible heartache—quite literally. In a panic, Tom rushed to an emergency room with chest pains and heart palpitations. The doctor said they were due to extreme anxiety and gave him a prescription for tranquilizers. But the drugs didn't work well enough, and a friend referred him to me.

I told Tom that rather than numbing himself, he needed to allow himself to grieve for the love and trust he had lost in such a wrenching way.

But Tom didn't want to face up to his sadness and emptiness, saying that "hurt too much." Instead, he declined therapy, resumed tranquilizers, and tried to escape by overdoing everything: working, traveling, drinking, gambling, eating, and dating.

Three years later, he came back to see me because he wanted to remarry, yet found himself unable to get close to his fiancée. But he still did not want to deal with his emptiness. Thus I was unable to help, and he broke the engagement.

YOU CANNOT FORGIVE AND REFORM YOUR LIFE WHILE YOU ARE RULED BY RESENTMENT, BITTERNESS, AND HURT.

You can't deny your emptiness, although a sad number of people try to do so.

What the Deceived Must Do

Allow yourself to regret the end of your old, untarnished relationship.

Do not, however, dwell in the past, sighing about how wonderful things used to be. Obviously, matters were *not* perfect, or no affair would have taken place!

Acknowledge both the good and bad aspects of the marriage and your contribution to each.

Understand that your spouse is hurting, too. It can be extraordinarily hard to abandon an affair. At the very least, your mate will miss the excitement, the uncomplicated passion and enjoyment—the feel-good, chocolate-cake aspects of extramarital love. What's more, he/she *will* feel guilt and sorrow for the pain inflicted on the spurned lover.

In most cases, a straying partner will feel agonizingly torn by love for both of you. When he protects the lover, he is really protecting a disowned part of himself. He perceives this as a last chance to redo his childhood, and that's why severing this relationship may indeed feel like losing an arm or a leg.

I am not suggesting the betrayed excuse the affair—just that they work to understand what caused it so that they may progress toward forgiveness and rebirth.

To revitalize the relationship, both parties must look back at their family patterns and forward to a new kind of loving. If you have always been a pursuer, for example, you will have to learn to distance yourself to recapture a runaway—as my parents and many of my patients did. Remember, there are aspects of a runaway hidden in you, too. If you pull back, you will be amazed to find the adulterer pursuing you.

The betrayed party must walk a thin line. *You must be willing to show your partner the door, but not shut it in his face. Be firm about the need to give up the lover, but make sure he knows how much* YOU *love him.* He needs to see that you are willing to work and to fight for the marriage and that you believe you will succeed. Deep down, he is terrified to choose the other, whom he doesn't know that well, and lose you forever.

Since you are not focusing on the adulterer, you *will* be lonely—reconnecting with your family of origin is a must and will help compensate for your pain.

What the Deceiver Must Do

First of all, you must **renounce** the adulterous affair in order to rebuild the marriage. No change in the relationship can occur as long as one partner keeps running to an escape hatch.

Let yourself **feel** your loss. Relinquishing that promise of a perfect, utopian union will intensify your feelings of emptiness and anxiety.

Face the damage you have done to the trust of not only your mate, but your children, parents, siblings, and friends.

You must **mourn** both your dead romance and your battered relationship, and grieve over the childhood wounds that led you into this mess. This is an excellent time for you, too, to do your family-of-origin work that you've been putting off.

This is difficult, depressing work, yet the adulterous partner must recognize the pain and uncertainty that has been inflicted and take responsibility. It is certainly cheaper and less painful than divorce, in any case—and you're never really divorced when children are involved.

TO CONFRONT OR NOT TO CONFRONT?

Should a betrayed partner ever meet the Other Woman or the Other Man?

It may sound like an invitation to mayhem, but *I believe that confrontation is sometimes justified*—if not in person, then at least over the telephone.

Confrontation can help in situations where the deceived is so obsessed with the lover that she/he cannot see the part they played in the deception, let alone think about forgiveness.

Meeting your rival gives you a realistic understanding of what you're up against. (Lovers are curious about you, too—that's why a surprising number are willing to talk.) You may be pleasantly surprised to discover that the competition is not as gorgeous or handsome as you fear—in many cases, as we've seen, the lover resembles the spouse.

A civilized contact can give the deceived partner back a measure of self-esteem and power. And doing it in the context of therapy can be very useful for keeping the contact constructive.

Confrontation can also help the betrayer who cannot make up his/her mind about ending an affair.

You should NOT consider a meeting, however, under these circumstances.
- If you are seeing a counselor together and making progress.
- If the deceiver is adamantly opposed.
- If either you or the lover has been making threats or has been verbally abusive.
- If you are still so angry that you fear you will not be able to control yourself. *Warning:* This could push the deceiver to the lover's side for good.

What if the affair is already over? Then there's no need for confrontation unless you're so fixated that you can't get the lover out of your mind.

Rules for Contact

When and if you do decide to make contact, these rules should apply:

1. Pick a neutral public place to meet or telephone.

2. *Never* humiliate the lover or your mate in front of friends, coworkers, children, or family members.

3. Tell the lover that you do not wish to hurt him/her, but you still love your partner and know the feeling is mutual.

4. Make it clear that you will fight for the relationship and that you and your spouse have a history together.

5. Ask for time to make it work. You might specify a period, say, two months, during which the lover will refrain from getting in touch with your partner while the two of you attend couples' counseling.

6. Point out that if your partner leaves the relationship still doubting and full of remorse, the lover will not get a fair shake—and might get hurt even worse later on.

7. Look your best.

8. **Remain cool but firm. Remember, these are peace talks.**

9. Try to see this person as a wounded child, too. Validate

his/her feelings, try to get him/her on your side, and get them to do the same.

10. Point out the negatives of your partner's situation—the children, the grim realities of maintaining two households.

But aim for empathy, not sympathy.

Lover's Lunch

One of the coolest customers I ever treated was Leonia. She was determined to win back her fifty-year-old husband, Bill, from his girlfriend, Tiffany.

While Bill dithered, she took action, setting up a lunch with the young woman. The dialogue went as follows: "I would like to put my marriage back on track. Could you give us a chance and leave my husband alone?"

"No. I love him. I know he's leaving you soon."

"Really? Well, in that case, may I share something?"

Leonia then calmly proceeded to lay out a few facts that Bill had never bothered to share with his young honey.

"His mother interferes in his life, and he supports her and sees her every Sunday and all the holidays. Our twin daughters are going to dental school—that's over $150,000 in tuition. I am keeping our $400,000 house and the style I am accustomed to."

Almost comically, Tiffany gaped, but Leonia wasn't through. "Also, did you know that he takes pills regularly for a heart condition and has a herniated disc which incapacitates him once or twice a year?"

It was all true, and all news to Tiffany.

Leonia never told Bill about her meeting, but she was not a bit surprised when her husband announced the following week that his affair was over. The couple worked hard in therapy, and Bill never rambled again.

Simone's Hollow Victory

Simone, in contrast, was a perfect example of how *not* to behave in this situation. When she found out about Walter's mistress, Andrea, she called her up and began shrieking insults.

Andrea, nevertheless, was patient. She urged Walter to return to his wife for three weeks to resolve any doubts.

No reconciliation was possible, however, because Simone only wanted to get revenge and voice her anger. She kept calling Andrea a whore to Walter and to the woman herself, over the telephone. The more she insulted Andrea, the closer Walter felt to his lover.

Simone turned every friend and relative she could against Walter and his woman. When I suggested this was not an ideal way to get him back, she declared "I feel better, I got it off my chest. This is the only thing that relieves my pain."

It was cold comfort, however. *Ironically, Walter was the son of an adulterer who didn't want to repeat the pattern and sought to reconcile.* As often happens, though, he was pushed to his lover's defense, and soon he felt obligated to stand by her. Simone was left with nothing but her sense of vindication.

Cerise, Zack, and Nan—All Together Now

On occasion, a lover will agree to meet with the couple to thrash though the issues. This is probably best done with a therapist unless you are all extremely civilized! They might discuss the pros and cons of continuing the affair, the impact on the family, what they find in the affair that they are not finding in their primary relationship.

In the case of Cerise, Zack, and his lover, Nan, all three wound up feeling better for the interaction.

Zack left Cerise for the younger woman, who proceeded to conduct a vendetta against her. Nan fanned his anger against Cerise so high that he never stopped to think about how much he missed his wife and his two children and how uncertain he felt.

The canny Cerise defused the situation by calling Nan. "Of course, I still love my husband and we miss him, but I understand that he loves you. I will not stand in your way, but please stop this vendetta because it is hurting my children. He is choosing you over them. There is room for them *and* you."

She then said to Zack, "We have not done the work we need to do, to grieve and feel sad for losing our life together after seventeen years. Don't hate me. It will affect your relationship with Nan and the kids.

"You can have her, but let's have a good relationship since we will have to talk again and again while the kids are young. Sure, I still love you—but I *will* let you go."

It became clear to Zack as Cerise spoke to Nan in front of him as well as on her own that she really did love him enough to release him. He came to see that Nan, in contrast, was possessive. Her adulterous father left home when Nan was little, and she was terrified of abandonment.

Simultaneously, Nan began to realize that she might be passing on the same painful legacy to Zack's children.

"I did to you what happened to me," Nan said, crying. The two women embraced and stopped regarding each other as enemies. Nan brought her estranged father into therapy, and reconciled with him. She stopped seeing Zack and began to date an available man for the first time.

And Zack, no longer being pulled apart and pursued by both women, decided that he loved Cerise and his family enough to join her in salvaging their marriage.

SURVIVAL TACTICS

Relationships which do not survive an affair may still involve partners who love one another, but pride or fear may get in the way of their ability to stay together.

Yes, the process is trying—in many ways, divorce can be easier.

Still, if you believe you can mourn a dead relationship and create a new one, then you probably can do it. My parents did it. Hundreds and hundreds of my patients have done it. What gets them through is not only my belief in them, but their belief in themselves. *You may need professional help, but your own attitude is crucial: with enough commitment, courage, and optimism, you can succeed.*

Here are five rules to grieve by—each starts with a letter that spells **GRIEF**.

GIVE yourself permission to be sad. You are entitled. The more you try to fight it, the longer it lasts. Seek help, though, if you feel suicidal or paralyzed by depression.

RESIST the exhortations of others to "Smile, you'll feel better," or, "Forget your troubles," "Don't worry, be happy."

INVEST time in mourning and each other. Do one of the exercises below every day.

ELIMINATE guilt, shame, and fear. Don't keep beating yourself with "if onlys." Don't expect yourself to function perfectly at work, school, or in your social life. Pretend you've had an operation and need time to recover.

FOCUS on the future. You are moving towards forgiveness and a reborn relationship. This, too, shall pass—when you are ready.

To help get you through this trying period, here are more patient-tested exercises:

MOPE TIME

It is perfectly natural to feel bleak when experiencing this. At the start, just going through the motions may be the best you can expect. If you normally have coffee at seven in the morning, have coffee then; if you normally eat dinner at six, stick to it. Routine helps.

You will feel bleak and blue, and have fears about dying and disasters. If you are so depressed that you can't get up in the morning; if you are abusing drugs or alcohol; or, if you are neglecting your job or your children, **you need professional help**. Seek it immediately.

Even if you feel you are functioning fairly well under the circumstances—*you wouldn't expect to run a marathon if you'd broken your leg*—set aside a specific "mope time" each day: at least one hour in the morning, and at least one hour at night. Allowing yourself to do this will make you feel more in control of your life...and get rid of some of your blues. Do this even if you think you don't need it. It will give you a specific time to mope instead of moping all the time.

Go ahead—watch tearjerkers, listen to sad songs (most love songs *are* sad, you'll notice), read weepy poetry or write some. And cry, cry, cry!

Go to Your Own Funeral

We've all longed to know what people would say about us after we were gone. This is our chance. It is also a tremendous opportunity to clarify our priorities, to break down our resistance to intimacy, to rescue our love.

No matter how awkward they may feel at first, I have never seen a couple go through this without being moved (be sure to keep tissues at the ready). This play acting forces the partners to confront the realities of what they have done and are about to do. The exercise demonstrates just what is at risk and underscores how little we value what we care about until we lose it.

Playing dead will help you make up your mind if you are trying to decide whether to work on the relationship or dissolve it and will help a straying partner choose between two lovers. Almost everyone opts to stay after they realize how much they would miss their partners and their future together. Even if you do decide to part, though, this exercise will help you forgive, which is critical to your emotional health.

1. The betrayed lies down and pretends to be dead. He or she closes his or her eyes and remains silent.

2. The betrayer approaches to say a last goodbye. He/she cites what *won't* be missed about the dear departed—the caustic arguments, the guilt, the resentments, the sensation of being trapped.

3. Next, the person explains what they *will* miss: the hilarious pancake breakfasts on Sunday mornings; the sexual highs; the birth of their first child; the hikes in the autumn woods.

4. Then the mourner expresses sorrow for the lost hopes, wishes, and dreams that will never come to pass: the round-the-world cruise they were going to take at retirement, their daughter's college graduation, growing old together.

5. The mourner expresses regrets for the affair and the pain it caused. Example: "Look what I did to you and the kids. I made a mess of our lives and now you're gone."

6. Finally, the mourner kisses his/her mate goodbye. With his own eyes closed, he or she visualizes this person gone forever. (By now, if love remains, the mourner will probably be crying openly.)

Wait at least a day before reversing roles so that both partners have time to sort through the deep emotions that have been stirred—and allow the betrayer to mourn the betrayed. Usually, no matter how angry they have been, both mates will be overwhelmed by how much they still love each other. *Note*: Oftentimes the adulterer can then give up the affair—the betrayed becomes a runaway and more dear. However, if the adulterer and betrayed break up, they are able to walk away with dignity for a future with another partner.

CAST THE LOVER AS THE CORPSE

In a variation on the funeral exercise, the betrayer bids farewell to the lover.

This should *never* be done in front of the betrayed spouse. The speaker will not be able to mourn honestly, and the onlooker will feel too raw to tolerate eulogies to a rival (and should not tolerate them).

If the lover is not willing to participate, the betrayer should perform the exercise with a surrogate—perhaps a friend, family member, or therapist. (As before, the estranged parent is the best option.)

The subject testifies to the dead lover about how sorry he/she is to say goodbye, listing the negatives and the positives of the affair. He/she asks forgiveness for abandoning the lover in order to reduce the residue of guilt and help forestall divorce later. Without the permission of the lover to let go it is almost impossible to return to the betrayed and achieve love and forgiveness. This exercise minimizes the lover and betrayer's communicating with each other after the affair has stopped.

Even if this does, indeed, become a memorial to their breakup (adulterer and lover)—as usually happens—both parties are able to walk away with dignity and heal much faster for a future with another partner.

If the adulterer still has a strong desire to return to the betrayed but can't, it is strongly recommended that a therapist be used in this exercise.

LOOK HOMEWARD

Both partners should do genograms first with one set of parents (see page 40) and then with the other, discussing the patterns that emerge and how they've shaped their own relationships. Remember: **You are not looking to pin the blame on your mothers and fathers but to understand the factors that contributed to your emptiness and theirs.** This will help strengthen the bond between you and detoxify your conflict. You can also chart forgiveness and grudgeholding patterns in your family.

YOU'VE GOT TO SEE A PATTERN TO CHANGE IT.

LIGHT A CANDLE

Since many religions use this as a remembrance of someone who has died, you two can light one in memory of your
old relationship. Blow it out, then light another for the start
of forgiveness and your new life together.

THINKING OF YOU

FOR ADULTEROUS PARTNERS
- Think of your lover three times a day as old and
  decrepit or cranky.
- After a month, think of the lover only once a day
  and only in negative terms.
- Think of your wife or husband as dead—how
  would you feel?

FOR BOTH PARTNERS (Adulterer and Betrayed)
- Think positive thoughts of each other three times
  a day when apart.
- Once a day, look deeply into each other's eyes for
  thirty seconds without talking.
- Twice a day, shower your mate with compliments
  and sweet nothings, to counter tensions and hostilities. This is surprisingly difficult, but essential.

OH, PROMISE ME

Once a week, renew your vow of fidelity to one another.

HAVE A SACKCLOTH-AND-ASHES DAY

Get in touch with your guilt. **Both parties have some.**
Write it down. Share the confessions with your mate. Do
penance—now but not forever.

Do a chore you've been promising to get to but keep
putting off, particularly if it involves physical exertion, like

scrubbing floors or scraping paint. You may feel cleansed by the effort.

HAVE A PLEASURE DAY

Try to make up for the stress you've been going through by doing whatever makes you feel pampered. Get a manicure or pedicure, a haircut, a massage. Buy a box of raspberries and eat every single one. Males may want to work out in the gym or buy a new stereo or computer.

Ask your mate to do you a favor—maybe to give you that massage.

CUDDLE UP

Cuddle twice a day for five to fifteen minutes. **Whenever you feel angry or resentful, hug instead.**

GIVE IT TIME

When you are ready to forgive, you will sense it. Don't push yourself. Keep doing the anger and the mourning exercises as needed with your partner and parents. Remember, **it is important to move on—but not so fast that you ignore these destructive emotions.**

Forging Forgiveness

Long after a lover has departed, destructive memories may linger on. Both sides may cherish their grievances and nurse their obsessions along.

Ellen, for example, seemed far more fascinated by her husband's former mistress than even *he* had ever been. Ages after Rod had ended the affair with Mary Ann, she'd press for the juicy details. "How often did you have sex with her? What did she like to do? How good was it for you?"

He couldn't win. If he didn't reply, she'd keep asking. If he did, she'd get hysterical and angry. The vicious circle went around and around. The more she demanded sympathy, the more he protected his lover; the more he did that, the worse Ellen felt—and the more sympathy she needed.

Ellen's insecurity and endless demands for reassurance were perhaps understandable: Her mother had played around with a vengeance, lied, and left her alone a lot as a child. She never gave her daughter any sympathy. Still, Ellen's obsession was ruining any chance at reconciliation the couple might have had—until I put these two hurt people through some exercises that allowed them to move beyond this point.

Ellen had to recognize that she had contributed to the decay of their marriage: she'd gained forty pounds after the birth of their second child and was preoccupied with raising the children. Lacking a healthy sense of self-worth, she didn't set boundaries for Rod, who came and went as he pleased and was not an involved father.

She finally took a stand, telling her husband that she knew he still loved Mary Ann, but if he wanted to preserve his marriage, he'd have to give up the affair. He did. By setting limits, she increased Rod's respect for her. By observing them, he gradually rebuilt her trust in him. **You can't control adulterers any more than you can control alcoholics, but you can establish standards of behavior.**

She was able to bury her obsession and diminish her nagging doubts. Making peace at last with her mother, she was able to obtain much of the solace she needed from that source.

When she stopped pressing him, he stopped being a reckless runaway, and they were able to forge forgiveness.

SECOND CHANCES

For such a generous people, Americans are remarkably stingy with forgiveness. *"I have my pride!"* they'll bluster. Or *"She doesn't deserve it!"*

"He's going to pay."

"She's not going to get off that easy!"

I don't believe, however, that forgiveness is something we bestow on someone else.

Rather:

FORGIVENESS IS A GIFT WE GIVE OURSELVES

Until we forgive the transgressor, we cannot get rid of our own anger, bitterness, and depression; we cannot feel hope and optimism. **Blame is an attempt to control the situation, but it actually keeps you stuck. Only when we reconcile can we start all over again.**

If you can recognize the aftermath of adultery as a second chance to work through your unresolved issues from childhood, you and your relationship could emerge in better shape than ever before.

Your ability to forgive depends on how well you have processed your denial, anger, mourning, and guilt.

As a child, you were caught in a triangle between your mother and father. *If you had siblings, you also triangulated with them.* You were always competing at home and in school. If you weren't chosen for a team in school, you were probably devastated and forlorn.

An affair reintroduces the triangle, the competition and betrayal. If your mate selects someone else, your self-esteem may be crushed. Your old insecurities (about being number one) are ready to rear up.

Handle them properly, though, and you could resolve issues you've struggled with your whole life. You must learn to recognize and work together on the wounded child in your mate and in your parents, as in yourself. You must recognize the patterns you inherited from your parents and learn to forgive their oversights and injuries that were accidentally inflicted on you. I find that adulterers usually change more than the betrayed so betrayed must be willing to look beyond their bitterness and change, too.

Forgiveness flows both ways. You must both ask for and give it as well.

To reach that state beyond blame and shame, you must pass through the following seven steps, whose initial letters spell **FORGIVE**. If you cannot, return to the anger or grief exercises until you feel ready to move on. *Ask for help again and again, from your parents, grandparents, and siblings, as well as from your mate.*

FORGET your obsession with the affair, no matter how tough it is to let go. This is just another way to put something or someone between you and your partner, another way to avoid intimacy and hide from your real problems.

OPEN your hearts to each other. Not only the affair, but other damaging secrets need to be revealed. Discuss your childhood fears and needs and emptiness as well.

REBUILD trust. To do this, the betrayer must not have any contact with the lover. Fight fairly, use conflict positively, share and confide. You will have doubts. Talk about them, don't fixate.

GO courting again. Renew your sense of fun, spontaneity, desire to please each other. Remember the traits that attracted you and cultivate them.

INVITE intimacy. Practice a new system of open, honest, full communication. Don't let work or children or in-laws or anything else reinsert itself between you. When your mate is forthright and it smarts, don't criticize—appreciate the honesty. Make it safe to communicate.

VALUE fidelity. Discuss your permissible limits, as in chapter 7. Repeat an oral contract to each other regularly, or even draw up a written one, as described on page 159.

ENCOURAGE embraces. From quick cuddles to the prolonged cradling prescribed in the previous chapter, touching and caressing will help ease the way over the most painful hurdle: sexual healing. People having affairs plan for sexual pleasure. Why shouldn't you?

TO THINE OWN SELF BE KIND

Most of us have deep dents and tears in our armor of self-esteem from our childhood. It's hard to extend our forgiveness to someone else while we are angry and disappointed in ourselves. Like Ellen, many of us feel we don't deserve fidelity and happiness.

So, before extending that hand, consider the following.

Practical Steps Toward Forgiveness

FORGIVE YOURSELF

1. Write a note.
   - Write "I forgive myself for the part I played in the affair."
   - Write the same message about your partner, your parent, and the lover. While doing so, visualize these persons as wounded children.
   - Write: "I forgive myself for hating one parent and siding with the other."
   - Write: "I forgive my parent for neglecting or betraying me because of his/her own emptiness."

Read the messages aloud three times.

2. Learn to love yourself.

Look in the mirror every morning and declare your worth. Convince yourself!

Say, "I'm lovable."
   - Recite the five best things about yourself to your mirror image and ask, "Why would anyone want to leave me?"
   - Hang up encouraging signs saying, for example: "I can work this out and I will," or "I deserve to be happy, I'm entitled."

Do these exercises when you wake up and right before you go to sleep. Don't be embarrassed if it seems superficial—you'll soon be feeling the words inside. **This really does work**.

3. Bury your obsession.

As we've seen, the betrayed sometimes become so fixated on and fascinated by the villainy of their partners that he/she lacks the time or energy to forgive. This is a cop-out; by hiding in victimhood, the injured partner doesn't have to confront what went wrong.

In the case of Ellen and Rod, I borrowed a little black magic from voodoo to teach her this symbolic exercise, so the marriage could survive.

She had discovered the affair when she found a sweater of Mary Ann's hidden under Rod's side of the bed. I had her wrap an old doll—representing Mary Ann—in it and then bury the whole package in the backyard. Whenever she feels she's about to bring up his ex-girlfriend and give vent to her mistrust again, she gazes at the "burial site" and meditates on the fact that the affair *IS* over, and her husband chose her.

See if you can do something similar. If you live in a city with no handy backyard—burn a picture of the lover or a phonebill or any letters you may have found. Whichever method you choose, tell yourself you are disposing of this unfortunate matter once and for all.

FORGIVE YOUR PARTNER

1. Make a Wish List

Expand the wish list of behavioral changes made on page 121 from three to ten.

Be as specific as possible. Instead of saying, "Don't be distant," say, "Tell me when the lover calls. I feel you won't be cheating then. Set limits and tell her/him you won't see her/him."

Trade lists and read carefully. Pick out at least three changes. Do not argue or engage in a power struggle. This is not negotiable and not a bartering system.

Remember, these changes will add to your credibility—and may change you for the better, too. The more you make, the more you increase trust between you; this is your chance to learn how to give.

THE LOVEPAT EXCHANGE

Each mate should make a list of twenty "lovepats" that will make him/her feel cherished. Include some already familiar, and find others you wish he/she would add. Some of them may sound frivolous, but this is the lifeline of revitalizing your relationship.

EXAMPLES:
- Call from the office to say "I love you" every day.
- Bring home flowers for me, even when it's not a special occasion.
- Remember our anniversary.
- Get up early to cook a special breakfast.
- Give me a card for no reason.
- Give me a backrub.
- Rent videos I love and you hate when I'm sick or feeling low.
- Remember what fragrance (perfume or after-shave) I wear and surprise me with some for no special reason.
- Make a special picnic and bring it to my office so we can have lunch on a beautiful day.
- Watch sports events with me.

2. State Your Limits (Don't misuse this or there will be no communication.)

Make a list of what you cannot or will not tolerate your partner doing. This is called taking a stand. *These are nonnegotiable.* Be sure to include flirtation if you have a problem with that; as we saw in chapter 7, the only acceptable boundaries are the ones you set honestly. Example: "Stop the affair or our relationship is over," or "Your lover has to stop calling the house or I'm leaving."

3. Draw up a Fidelity Contract

Put your limits into a formal contract, the way Carl and Marsha did, whom you met in Chapter 1. *The best time for such a contract is before you live together, but it's never too late.*

Both were scared adult children of adulterers, and theirs was the most icily polite marriage I've seen in my entire practice. At one point, after Carl, a minister, ran off with Marsha's best friend, I urged them to fill out "scorecards" of their grievances.

Carl's was a mile long. "She never came to hear me preach on Sundays. When I played in a chamber music group, she never came to hear me. The house is never clean enough."

He had mentioned none of these grievances to Marsha. Her scorecard, meanwhile, was practically empty. She excused everything, she wouldn't set limits—she'd get mad at me instead!

Eventually, however, she let him go with his lover, mourned, and got on with her life. Carl, however, acted like a classic runaway and after a year wanted to come back.

After much soul-searching, Marsha took him back...but only with a contract. He understood that if he cheated again, there would be no reprieves.

Sample Contracts*
For the Adulterer

I, _____, give my word that if I enter into any adulterous relationship, I give up the right to have you as my partner. There are no reprieves, no discussions, and no second chances.

If I have an uncontrollable urge, I will enlist the help of my therapist and my partner to resist it, rather than act it out. I promise to work on our relationship, which I value, instead of running.

Signed, _____
(the former unfaithful partner)

For the Betrayed

I _____agree that if my partner is unfaithful to me, I will not accept any excuses or promises to change.

---

*These samples are for someone who has had several affairs. The wording would differ for specific situations. Review and discuss your fidelity contract frequently.

There are no more second chances. Our marriage will
end in divorce.

However, I will not be judgmental or critical if my
partner verbalizes a desire to stray. Understanding that
this could represent some change taking place in my
partner, and that I may have contributed to the situation, I will do everything I can to help save this relationship.

Signed, _____
(former betrayed partner)

Forgive Your Parents

As already emphasized, I believe it is imperative to reconnect to your parents if you want to remake your relationship.

Anger dissipates when you see the deceiver as a wounded
child, especially if that deceiver is your parent. Although I
had built up a great deal of hostility toward my father, it
melted away when I witnessed him reduced to tears in Dr.
Fogarty's office. For the first time, he was no longer my
enemy. My mother and I were able to move along to
forgiveness. *She had to learn to forgive her father, too.* Dr.
Fogarty said, "If you don't bridge the distance with your
fathers, you will not be able to completely trust and love."

Gradually, she and I came to realize that we had frozen out
my dad for years to punish his philandering. His isolation, of
course, only encouraged him to continue to look elsewhere
for love. **He, too, needed a rapprochement with the mother
who had wounded him.**

My father forgot it when, after a psychoanalytic therapy
session, I told him I hated him. The words cut sharply,
especially because he hated himself, too, for the shameful
things he'd done. When we began to talk honestly to each
other, I asked him to forgive those words that had hurt for so
many years.

Enlist your parents as allies in your struggle to deal with your emptiness and mend your relationship. They can support you as no one else can.

What about so-called toxic parents?

I certainly do not advocate that you spend time alone with a parent who abused you as a child. You may, however, be able to put some of your pain to rest if you see him/her in a safe, supervised setting, or contact such a parent by mail or telephone. You cannot hope for closeness, which is intense and takes time and effort over years, but you can hope for a connection.

My patients sometimes quote other therapists who advise them to disconnect and reject the parent who abused them, so that they do not relive the pain. I don't agree. Out of sight does not mean out of mind, and emptiness is too excruciating to bear alone. You need to share it with your parent, whenever possible, as well as your partner for true healing.

In some cases, you may discover that you have been wrong about the offending parent all these years.

One patient of mine had been raised by her furious mother to hate her divorced father, who had supposedly been an adulterer.

When she contacted me because she kept getting involved with married men, I urged her to bring her father in. They hadn't spoken in twenty years.

Once they did, she discovered that he had never really wanted to leave. He insisted that his involvement with a colleague had been largely emotional. He had been lonely in his marriage because his wife was aloof, but he had never slept with another woman. Meanwhile, he had longed to see his daughter every day of his life.

She forgave him and with his help is learning to trust other men.

Reconnecting With Distant Parents

To reach out and touch these enormously important people:

1. Write a separate letter from the heart to each of your parents. You may or may not send these to them, but you should read them to your mate. Discuss what you wish could have been different about their actions during your childhood. Mention the positive experiences, too, and ask them for forgiveness.

2. Write yourself letters that you would have liked them to write to you. "They" ask for forgiveness.

3. Schedule some outings with the parent who angers you most or from whom you are most distant. Keep it brief—no heavy heart-to-heart talks yet. Be sure to ask the permission of the parent to whom you're closest. Stay in touch with this parent, too, and keep him/her informed of what takes place.

Pick something you know your parent likes. Don't do what I did, dragging my father to dinners and museums. I was happy, he was bored, until I finally started taking him to his favorite pursuits: bowling and sporting events.

Don't confront the parent—just cultivate the family tie.

4. If you feel that both of you can handle the situation, tell your parent that you are having trouble with your mate because of some unfinished business from childhood. Don't blame the parent. Instead connect in a meaningful way and ask for help with your problems. Give "strokes" and let your parent know you understand he/she did the best that was possible under the circumstances. After a connection is formed, on some visits, bring your partner so partner and parent may share in the healing and forgiveness process.

5. Do a genogram with them. Ask the parent whether there is adultery in the family background, other betrayals, abandonment, grudge-holding. Emphasize that you are doing this not to shame or blame, but to heal your wounds and theirs.

6. If your parent has died, visit the cemetery or a favorite spot and meditate on this subject. Put your feelings in a letter and read it aloud. Tell your parent that you are having trouble because of emotional scars you developed growing up, then ask for help. Forgive and ask for the parent's forgiveness.

Share your letter with your mate and with the parent who survives or, if both are dead, with your mate's parent.

7. Do the "embraceable you" exercise (page 120) with the parent from whom you're most distant. Bring your partner along occasionally for this exercise.

You can't get what you need from a mate or give until you resolve these issues with your parents. Often it turns out that this connection is what the unfaithful partner has been seeking all along from lovers...and never finding.

Finally, MOVE ON. As noted, it's destructive to fixate on the affair or to wallow in recriminations.

1. FIND FUN

Many couples have forgotten how to enjoy each other. They resist, they feel guilty, and they have a great deal of difficulty experiencing pleasure.

"We're too old for that," they say.

Or, "I can't get away from the job/kids." Or, "Won't we look silly?"

You've got to rediscover your childlike joyfulness, though, if you want to rejuvenate your marriage.

Make a list together of the things you used to do together, or always wanted to do, as well as the things you each enjoyed as children. Yes, the list will usually include several things your spouse did with the lover. So what? Better you than the competition.

Try at least five. Make it a priority. **Remember: When it comes to revitalization, fun is serious**. Structure time.

Decide that on Mondays or Fridays you will have an enjoyable date every week.

- Go ice skating/roller skating.
- Take mambo lessons.
- Go canoeing.
- Dine out or picnic together once a week.
- Go to a concert and hold hands.
- Dunk strawberries in chocolate fondue.

2. STORE UP SURPRISES

Make a similar list but keep it secret. Dip into it once a week or so.

Each partner should try to appreciate and enjoy whatever turns up. **It's surprisingly hard for recipients to accept these tokens of love. Don't criticize the choices or say, "I don't need that."**

- Call up your partner for a date on the spur of the moment.
- Kidnap your spouse for the weekend or even a week. Pick him/her up after work with a bag all packed.
- Tuck some home-baked cookies into his/her briefcase.

3. WHISPER SWEET NOTHINGS

Twice a day, for thirty seconds, tell your mate small, positive things. "I love the way your hair falls in your eyes...the way you laugh." "That was a great dinner you made last night." Most Americans have trouble with this exercise. Don't be Scroogey. You can certainly find something positive to say—about the way they walk, drive, or whatever. It all helps cancel out the resentments that may linger. This is a quantum leap toward forgiveness.

4. RESTORE SIZZLE

You've got to turn up the heat in your physical relationship. (**Warning:** Runaways may feel uncomfortable and try to sabotage these efforts. Keep trying.)

- Dress up in costumes, if that's something one or the other of you has always secretly fantasized.
- Neck in the back seat of your car.
- Stay in a motel room with a waterbed and jacuzzi, and watch the X-rated videos.
- Try new positions, sex toys...whatever you don't find repugnant.
- Try that old standby, a joint bubblebath by candlelight.

Caution: As you may remember, you two are intimacy-avoiders, so pursuers beware—you, too, may become a runaway when restoring sizzle.

5. TRADE PLACES

To give the betrayed a sense of regained control over the relationship, put an entire weekend day and evening of fun and play in his/her hands. You promise to do whatever is suggested.

Reverse places the next day, so you feel a sense of power, too.

No complaining allowed. If it's a baseball game and you hate baseball, try to enjoy your mate's enjoyment. Bring a paperback, go get lots of refreshments, or simply throw yourself into the spirit of things. No "guilting" allowed. Give in, compromise, enjoy! Your turn comes tomorrow.

6. SCHEDULE FIRESIDE CHATS

No matter how reassured you are, some pain will almost inevitably remain. Make an appointment to discuss it on a regular, time-limited basis with your partner and your parents both in a group and individually. Go slowly at first until trust returns. Cradle each other, talk about your fears of abandonment rather than making accusations. **Tie today's fears into yesterday's hurts.**

At first, do this daily; then weekly; then monthly—as forgiveness takes hold.

Forgiveness must be refreshed to stay alive...just like relationships.

Jim and Tessie's Curative Touching

Testimony to the curative power of touching and talking can be found in the case of Jim and Tessie. In their own way, they loved each other dearly, although they had not had sex for ten—yes, ten—years.

Tessie, a librarian and the mother of four, was an undiagnosed manic depressive, given to the enormous mood swings of her condition. Jim, a journalist, sought refuge from her moodiness in the arms of others; in seven years, he had six affairs with women he met at work.

Our job was monumental, but we chipped away at it, little by little. Tessie was finally convinced to see a psychiatrist so she could control her condition with medication. Finally, she began to open up about her anguish when she had lost her father at the age of three. To make matters worse, her mother had been deaf and unable to communicate well. In this case, all four parents were gone.

I asked the couple to do the "embraceable you" exercise (page 120) only twice a week at first (because it was scary for them both), then twice a day. Tessie was instructed to tell Jim how she longed to be with her father again, to know whether he really loved her. Jim was to nurture her, comfort her, and flood her with compliments, while holding her on his lap, telling her, "I love you, you're special."

Jim had been distant and reserved, compounding her hurt and fear about everything. In their daily embraces, they began to bond. He healed himself, too, learning to become as affectionate as he had always secretly wanted to be.

Slowly, their sexual feelings began to return.

Not long ago, I received a card from them. It was their thirtieth anniversary, she said, and she wanted to thank me—they had never felt so close.

• 13 •

Sexual Healing

Most couples hit the most treacherous stretch on the road to reconciliation AFTER the affair is over.

Intellectually, they may both understand that the interloper is gone, but emotionally and sexually they just can't forget.

So it was with George and Ariel. She found out about his affair in a typical catch-me-if-you-can manner: She discovered a lacy silk teddy that did *not* belong to her kicked under her side of their bed.

She confronted; he confessed. But months, even years after the affair ended, it unreeled endlessly in her mind.

"I can't bear for you to touch me," she told him. "I cringe every time you touch my hair, my face." It was bad enough that he had made love to another woman, she thought—but the fact that he had done this in their marital bed made it unbearable.

SEXUAL HEALING

Sexual healing is often the most difficult part of forgiving, and the part we have the most trouble talking about. Without realizing it, we resist sex to put off intimacy.

168

We are at our most vulnerable during sex. Some of us had sexual problems before adultery occurred—although, as we've seen, that's rarely the only reason.

But even if our sexual relations were good, a lot of us simply can't stop replaying our tapes. We can't get over our distaste for sleeping with the enemy.

Again and again, I hear the same painful monologues from patients, the ones they rerun whenever they even *think* about having sex with the unfaithful partner.

- *"How could you have slept with both of us and still looked our kids in the eye? What if you have AIDS?"*
- *"I feel dirty. You repulse me. What else are you lying about? I can't be naked with you ever again. I'm exposed, I have no defenses. You have stripped my dignity.*
- *"I can't ever lie in your arms and feel safe.*
- *"We both know you're thinking of her—and that perfect, Playmate body."*

In truth, he may *not* be thinking of her; it may be that only *you* keep dragging the former paramour into your bed.

It's time for her to go, and it's time for you to resume or remake a relationship that will improve your lives in every way.

How?

Fascination Versus Fixation

Our fascination with illicit sex is only natural. We can't help but recall the forbidden thrills of the teenage years when sneaking around added spice to sex.

It's also natural for the betrayed to display curiosity about the competition. The matter should be discussed after it becomes known, because it demystifies and detoxifies the fantasy. Adulterous partners should allow betrayed partners to ask the following questions:

- How often was there sex? How often did you see the person?
- How long did the affair last?

- What was the reason for the affair?
- Where did assignations take place?
- Who else knows?
- Is it over?
- Were or are you in love?

Often, the answers can be comforting.

Lannie was convinced that Gerard's lovemaking with his mistress, Candy, had been much better than it was with her. In therapy with the three of them, however, it emerged that Gerard had often been impotent with Candy. "He loves you," the Other Woman said. "I just didn't want to admit it. You were in OUR bed." (For more on confrontations and when they can help, see Chapter 11, "Grieving and Goodbyes.")

Beware, however, when legitimate fascination turns to fixation, which can result when the betrayer provides too much detail.

After Howie found an audiotape of his wife and her lover talking sexy, he made the mistake of asking her to tell him everything. Worse, she did—and now he's too self-conscious to make love to her.

Charles, meanwhile, compared and contrasted his girlfriend, Debra, to the woman he'd slept with at a sales convention. Debra was not inspired to try any of the sexual tricks he described.

Lois called Ronnie's mistress, Mira, for details of their lovemaking. Mira, wanting to break them apart, described just when and where and how they'd done it, including a stretch limousine and the kitchen floor.

Lois later learned that half of what she heard was pure—or impure—fantasy. Still, to this day she has not regained her trust in Ronnie.

You don't want or need to know every position they tried, whether she stripteased for him, whether she had stretchmarks, what their favorite song was. You may think you want to know—*but it will simply give you more to have to forget.*

How can you get through this trying period?

STOP PUNISHING YOURSELF

Don't abstain. If you are refusing to sleep with your mate to punish him/her, you are really punishing yourself.

Why deprive yourself of something as satisfying as an orgasm? I remind you once again: *Forgiveness is a gift you give yourself—especially in the sexual arena.*

If you have decided—and too many do—that you will not sleep together ever again, why stay together? Either forgive, take pleasure in each other again, or move on.

Don't settle for an asexual relationship and rationalize that it is safest. Eventually, it will be dangerous. You will be resentful, and affairs can resurface. On the other hand, while you struggle with real issues, sex can speed the healing process.

TAKE CHARGE

Tell yourself you will have sex, that you want and need sexual pleasure. Remind yourself that you are no longer a kid who thinks sex is a dirty, shameful, guilty act. Instead of the self-destructive sort of monologue you've seen above, give yourself a PEP TALK before sex. Tell yourself something like this:

"I refuse to stop myself from sexual pleasure anymore. I deserve joyfulness again. Why should someone else benefit from all my hard work in this relationship, what we built together, our family, our old age together?

"I will rise above the fear of her coming into our lives again. I'll talk to him when I'm scared to make love because of it and ask him to hold me. I'll hold him when he feels scared if the sexual feelings won't return for him.

"I won't withhold sex like I do now, because it lets her win."

CULTIVATE YOUR SEX APPEAL

Reward yourself for not continuing your obsession by doing whatever makes you feel sensual. Women should get a pedicure, a massage, a new hairdo, some of that sexy lingerie you've coveted but never bought. Men should buy new colored underwear, new aftershave, or try a hair replacement. But most of all, get a good attitude. *Those who encourage themselves to feel sexy are sexy.*

Flo, for example, transformed her fear of losing her husband into a newfound sensuality. No, she didn't wrap herself in plastic wrap and greet him at the door. But when she found out that the sex hadn't been dynamite in his outside relationship, she determined that theirs *would* be. She decided to concentrate on touching and listening to him more—and she became sexier and sexier as their sex life improved!

▸ Use the scare of adultery as you would a brush with death, to remind you that life is short, so you'd better take advantage of it.

▸ Set up a structure and time to pleasure each other—the unfaithful do.

Here are some exercises that some of my patients have used to get their sex lives going again.

Many involve so-called mind-games that, indeed, may seem unnatural to you. But then again, you're already playing negative games if your mind is running destructive images over and over. Why not change the tape?

Mind-games can work for, as well as against, your sexual relationship, provided you don't scrutinize your feelings to death.

BATHING BEAUTY

Larry refused to have sex with his wife, Lorna, after she had an affair. He said he felt inadequate as a lover in comparison to her paramour. I realized, however, that he also regarded her as unclean.

I suggested the two participate in a variation on a Mikvah, the ritual bath of orthodox Judaism. Before a bride marries, she is cleansed by other women in a communal ceremony.

Instead, Larry bathed Lorna in a sensual bubblebath. He felt emotionally close to her, she felt purified of her guilt. She forgave his possessiveness, and he took steps to understand why she had fled and to forgive her.

ACTING AS IF...

To revive their sexuality, I always tell patients to act as if they felt confident and sure.

Overanalysis can kill off your tentative sexual feelings just as they start to sprout again.

Yes, this *is* an artificial sensation...at least, at first. But breaking any bad habit feels that way initially. If you want to change, you must do what *works*, not what's comfortable.

In one case, the errant husband was profoundly moved when his wife initiated sex. When Pete married Louisa, he felt he wasn't that important to her. Now, her generous lovemaking has convinced him otherwise. He knew the effort was trying for her because she kept picturing his curvaceous young lover. Yes, their first encounter was tense. But the second time, he went out of his way to repay her with attentiveness—and she had an orgasm.

GET TO KNOW YOUR BODIES AGAIN

If you're acting as awkward as teenagers, you might as well enjoy the sensation. *Think of yourselves as virgins again.*

Try some instructional books and videos. Discuss fantasies you've never revealed. Talk about what it would take for you to feel cherished again sexually. Increase the amount of caressing, kissing, holding that you do. As we saw with Jim and Tessie, the couple who had not made love for ten years, affection alone can begin the Big Thaw.

Rhonda, for example, told her husband, Jordan: "Let's learn again, like new lovers. Let's act like virgins. It really is the first time in our new relationship that there is no one or nothing in the middle—not your girlfriend, not work, not our children, not in-laws, not money. That is so new, yet so scary."

PLAY A NEW TAPE

Instead of seeing that steamy scenario starring The Other, visualize one starring you and Your Mate.

- Pretend the two of you are lying on a float in the blue Caribbean, bobbing gently in the waves. Or maybe you're floating on a cloud in an azure sky. You both close your eyes and feel safe. Then you make mad, passionate love. No one else is around—you feel totally uninhibited, there is no anger, only passion and forgiveness.
  You are free—to start a new life and love.
- Picture yourself on your honeymoon—*what you did for love*. Remember that you were the one he chose. Remember all the things about you that he has complimented.
- Imagine that this is the last time you will ever see each other. Maybe this is *Casablanca*—and one of you is about to get on that last plane out. Yes, this is contrived—but it might add an electrifying energy to your lovemaking and enable you to forget your self-consciousness.

DON'T WAIT FOR THE "RIGHT" MOMENT

There's never a *right* or *perfect* moment to resume sex. Ashley and Samantha had waited for three years after their reconciliation when they came to see me. I told them that if they waited any longer, their relationship might be permanently frozen.

Ashley said his therapy group had suggested he move into another bedroom.

"How will that help you to trust one another again?" I asked. "That is only more rejection. Take each other's hands, look into each other's eyes.

"There is a reason the rubber band of your relationship did not break—you came back together for a reason."

By now, both were crying. I asked why. "I love her, but I'm frozen inside," he said. "We had sexual problems before." "It's my fault," said Samantha, whose affair had precipitated the separation. When I asked why she picked someone who was so sexually low-key, she confided that she had been sexually abused by her father as a child.

She had told Ashley this. Now she said, "I picked him because he was gentle, not aggressive like my father."

Eventually, they came to realize that she had sought refuge in an affair because, paradoxically, it seemed safer. Making love with her husband, someone she was close to, reminded her of her incestuous experiences.

Ashley, meanwhile, was horrified to learn about her abuse. He felt he had no right to make sexual demands that might terrify her. Samantha needed to feel safe with Ashley before she could trust him and make love. But she also needed him to move beyond the polite passivity that she only *thought* she wanted.

Together, they began to search for a place of emotional safety where they could meet. I suggested to Samantha, "He can still be gentle, yet express his feelings for you."

One day, they showered together—she wore her bathing suit. Ashley suddenly comprehended the depth of her shame. "I thought you didn't like the way I made love, but you don't like the way you look and feel!" he said. Then he added, soothingly, "You're so pretty and I missed you when I left you. I want to be intimate with you. Help me," he said.

"Help me," she replied. "I remember my father."

Gradually, they helped each other.

At first, they held and stroked each other in the dark, so that he would not have to look at her "shameful" body. Then,

one night, she let the moonlight stream through a window.
Soon after, they called me: they had made love at last.

Tired of the discouragement and the excuses and the pain,
they had simply led each other to where they wanted to be.
She did not think of her father, and he did not think of his
former lover.

They got there by following some advice my mother often
gives: **"If the light switch is off, take each other's hand and
find it together."**

You can do it, too—and not necessarily by doing what
comes naturally.

A Passionate Postscript

For much of this chapter, we've talked about what it takes
to heat up a marriage sexually. One of the best ways to make
sure it never cools down is to keep it warm emotionally.

As noted in the chapters on anger, grief, and forgiveness,
you must hold each other, talk, and listen to each other if you
are to renew trust.

The same is true for passion.

*Remember, in many cases an affair is a dysfunctional attempt to
stabilize a marriage. When the other lover disappears, so does this
smokescreen. You must tend to the marriage beneath.* If you took
your partner for granted, you may be one of those who needs
to learn to love more, as my father did. If you were the one
who was taken for granted, you may have to learn to love your
partner less and yourself more, as my mother did.

RELATIONSHIPS THAT SURVIVE AFFAIRS HAVE ABIDING
EMOTIONAL AND PHYSICAL BONDS. THESE COUPLES GEN-
UINELY LIKE EACH OTHER AND HAVE BUILT A HISTORY
TOGETHER. THIS TRUE INTIMACY IS NOT ACCIDENTAL; IT
IS CULTIVATED EVERY DAY.

Here are some ways to strengthen your relationship and
keep infidelity at bay:

1. *Express your love verbally every day.*
   Say "I love you," and compliment your partner. Appreciate his/her virtues. (See "sweet nothing" exercise, page 164). Don't presume that because you have been together so long, he or she can read your mind and knows that you admire his wit or diligence. Say it out loud and often.
2. *Express your love physically every day.*
   Do this not just through sex, but through frequent embraces and touches. (See "embraceable you," page 120).
3. *Don't expect perfection—in yourself or your mate.*
4. *Don't retreat into wounded silence or sulk—communicate.*
   Remember that peace is not worth any price.
5. *Learn to express anger appropriately.*
   (See chapter 9.) Don't attack, be contemptuous or supercritical—three traits that characterize couples headed for divorce (unless fighting fairly with bulletproof vests).
6. *Maintain a positive attitude about change in the relationship.*
   Change is inevitable. Resolve to grow together.
7. *Make the relationship a priority.*
   Structure time to be alone together, enjoying and nurturing your relationship.
8. *Confide and share.*
   Be the deepest of friends, willing to share your worst anxieties as well as your greatest triumphs. Cheer for each other, and tell each other secrets you could not—and would not—reveal to anyone else.

Researchers have identified many common factors about marriages that end in divorce. They include repetitive, hurtful criticism, contempt, and coldness. Take care that this does not describe you.

• 14 •

Saving the Children Through Family Play Therapy

Ralph came from a long line of lady-killers. His grandfather and father, both successful clothing manufacturers, had even been known to swap mistresses when they tired of them.

Ralph married a lissome showroom model, Cynthia, but saw no reason to forego the family tradition any more than the family business. After his third affair in seven years of marriage, though, Cynthia moved out with their son, Ralphie. She swore her child would not repeat the pattern.

Then Ralphie had a nearly fatal asthma attack, which doctors said was largely psychosomatic. When he emerged from the oxygen tent, his anxious parents, united by his illness, said they'd give him whatever he wanted. His wish, of course, was that they get back together.

Ralph and Cynthia promised to try—and talked Ralphie's grandfather and great-grandfather into it, too. After several months of four-generation therapy, the couple was finally able to recognize their destructive family pattern—and the entire family was able to break it. They, and Ralphie, are fine.

Quite often, when a family comes to me for help, a little child has led them. **In their innocent forthrightness, children express what a family suppresses. If you want to see how well you're dealing with your emptiness, take a look at your children.**

Remember, children tend to think in magical ways. They believe they are omnipotent: "If I wish it, it will happen." Therefore, they also blame themselves for the bad things that happen, and tell themselves that if they apply the right hocus-pocus, they can put Humpty Dumpty—or their folks—back together again.

Like gamblers, adults involved on both sides of affairs never outgrow this magical thought process. "If I pretend this doesn't exist, it will go away/have no consequences," they tell themselves.

The little ones, meanwhile, say to themselves, "Daddy doesn't love me. He's with his girlfriend again. Daddies should be with their children." Or they ask, "Are we getting a new daddy? What did I do wrong?" Sometimes their desire to fix things makes them incredibly brave: One youngster walked up to his father's mistress and told her to leave his dad alone. He was unbearably conflicted about his loyalties: Should he tell his mother about this woman?

Frequently, behavioral symptoms signal that something is amiss. These may include failure to sleep or to eat, bed-wetting, poor conduct, fighting with siblings, failing grades, withdrawal, or hyperactivity. In a family, though, there's no such thing as a problem in just one person, no matter how it looks.

As discussed, such problems are especially likely to surface during transition periods, such as the arrival of a new baby or the death of a grandparent. They may also freeze a child at a certain developmental stage. If a child had the normal difficulty separating from the parent to go to school, for example, that may be exacerbated to the point of hysteria if the child is abandoned by an adulterous parent.

If a child is at the Oedipal stage of development—when he/
she is strongly identified with the same-sex parent and in love
with the one of the opposite sex—an affair is especially
traumatic. Not only does the child have to share the parent
with another parent, but with yet another rival, the lover.
This sets the stage for confusion about intimacy later in life.

As we've seen in chapter 3, *even very young children sense the
emotional turmoil their parents are experiencing. In fact, their
behavior can even signal adultery when a parent doesn't know
what's going on.* **If you try to hide your problems from your
children or lie to them, you can make matters even worse.
The kids grow up not trusting you.** All of us fear abandonment, and betrayal is the ultimate abandonment.

In many cases, troubled children do not display symptoms.
This can be even more dangerous. To unlock these secret
hurts, I put together two existing forms of therapy to create
Family Play Therapy.

Traditionally, play therapy without the family has been
used in individual child psychoanalysis, dealing with sibling
rivalry, abuse, and other serious problems. I find that Family
Play Therapy is more useful with adults and children, especially when treating adultery. Even children too young—or
too inarticulate, or resistant such as teenagers—to benefit
from traditional family therapy will open up when play is
added. **Play is to children what conversation is to adults.**

Family Play Therapy is like an emotional X-ray, not just for
the child but for the parents. This is a joint effort between
them. It frees the child from the burden of keeping a secret,
and it minimizes adult shame and guilt. Recalling the freedom of their own childhoods, grown-ups may deal more
easily with their own fears and anger. Family Play Therapy
expedites the stages of mourning and forgiveness for adults
as well as children suffering from adultery. (From Eaker Weil,
"Unlocking the Family Secret in Family Play Therapy.")

Family Play Therapy is:

- honest

- nonthreatening
- equalizing (*It allows parent and child to communicate on the same level.*)
- useful (*A child can show how she feels with dolls even if she can't tell it.*)
- helpful (*It teaches parents what the child really knows about family problems.*)
- supportive (*It allows the child to know what is going to happen and how to deal with the unknown.*)

Families must be willing to stick with the therapy even after symptoms are arrested, however.

Her parents brought in five-year-old Shawna because she was wetting the bed. When that stopped, as she overcame the fear that Dad would leave because Mom had a new lover, the family dropped out of therapy. Her mother also ended the affair. Since they still hadn't resolved their deeper problems, I was not surprised when they came back one year later. This time, Dad was having an affair, and their nine-year-old son, David, was flunking school. This time the whole family remained in therapy for six months. *As often happens, the symptoms simply shifted from person to person until the underlying problems were addressed.*

Many adults who feel they're only doing Family Play Therapy for the kids wind up having a good time and solving their own oftentimes three-generational problems. Fun brings out their own inner child, and can help save all the children from repeating this dangerous pattern.

Family Play Therapy can be done between you and your child without a therapist. Do not attempt this, however, if
a) child abuse is involved;
b) one or both parents are likely to strike out or blow up at the child or each other (if you haven't worked out your rage, you may lay it on your children and scare them);
c) one or both has a hot temper or a record of substance abuse.

How to Heal Through Play

What you will need

Equipment:
Crayons, watercolors or chalks, paper, a blackboard, or easels are helpful.

For kids ages three to eleven, dolls, two dollhouses, hand puppets, miniature furniture, and small figures are useful. (I use the popular and inexpensive "Little People."). So are clay, punching bags, a cobbler bench with wooden hammer and nails, Lincoln Logs, drums, toy guns.

For older children, including teens, checkers or Monopoly or other board games may be used. (I've had luck with the "Gilligan's Island" game from Playskool, named for the 1960s series about a group of castaways on a deserted island. It permits kids and parents to express the feelings of ostracism that adultery often provokes.)

Pets can be useful. In therapy, one nonverbal girl could only reveal her father's sexual molestation by saying her little puppy was afraid of Dad.

Make a fun grab bag full of small toys, which can include some the child already owns. Have the youngster close his/her eyes and pick three items. Then you start a story about one new item (structured toward adultery). If the child continues the story he/she gets to keep the toy. You finish it, and supply the moral about adultery.

Schedule
Set aside at least ten minutes at the same time every day to play intensively. You will be able to tell a lot by your child's changing anger, anxiety, or other attitude. Often, this is the only positive attention a child gets in this difficult family situation. (The more distant parent must do this for ten minutes a day, especially if this parent is a runaway.)

Ground Rules

The child must be allowed to say anything without fear of reprisals.

- No secrets are allowed.
- No anger from you is allowed, no reprimands later. No "that's bad!" judgments.
- Do what the child wants. Read a story, play ball. Allow for the rules to be changed. Your child is in control (except for safety considerations).
- Don't worry about messes.
- Don't overwhelm the youngster with too many toys or too much stimulation at once.
- Be comfortable, flexible, and patient. Wear old clothes so you can get right down on the floor and be at the child's level.
- If appropriate, enlist the grandparents. The child heals faster if they're there—and so may you.

NOTE: In my practice, I sometimes do Family Play Therapy with two or three families at once. Families take turns playing and telling their stories. This forms an adultery support group in which families can comfort and reassure each other that they are not alone.

- Encourage the use of whatever makes children relax. One boy brought his clarinet to one of my support groups; another brought his hamster.
- Remember that reassurance is essential. Be lavish with hugs, special treats, "I love you's."
- Never lie. Don't promise something you can't give, such as a reconciliation.

Here are some specific exercises—and some inspiring cases of the families who used them successfully.

DRAW A FAMILY TREE

This is a child's version of the genogram. Fill in not only names and faces, but also pets and favorite toys. Leave a space for the lover. Triangulate relationships—indicate who is close to whom, who fights, etc.

The parent needs to get things going by asking pertinent, adultery-related questions: Where is Mommy during the day? What do you like most about Mommy? Where does Daddy go at night? Are you like Daddy in any way? The results can be surprising. Even the very young child may fill in a lover on the family tree, although the family believes they've kept the secret.

FOR EXAMPLE:

Len and Judy were certain they had sheltered their daughter, Stepanie, five, from discord over her father's affair. The two, both doctors, never argued or spoke about it in front of her, after all, and tried to put on a happy face. Still, she started having nightmares.

I asked her to draw a picture of her family, and she did: mother, father...and a second lady in between.

DRAW YOUR FEELINGS

On a sketch pad or blackboard, draw both happy and sad faces to show the ambivalent feelings that Mommies and Daddies and children have about falling in love with someone else and the possibility of separation and divorce.

PLAY HOUSE

Using two doll houses and a selection of boy and girl figures, ask your child who lives in the houses and where everyone is located right now. Have an extra doll to represent the lover in case the child wants to put the interloper in. If the child mentions the paramour, introduce the doll: "This is Daddy's friend." If you aren't sure whether the child knows, the extra doll will often elicit the truth.

See whether the youngster keeps dolls close or distant—you can learn a lot about your family relations.

Jennifer, age three, dropped a real bombshell of a story with the dolls. She had been brought in because she was clinging to her parents, refusing to go to nursery school. It turned out the poor girl had not only figured out that Daddy had a girlfriend, had been introduced to her and asked to keep it a secret from Mommy, which made her feel disloyal.

One weekend, her father, Ted, had taken her on a three-hour drive to meet his paramour, Brittany. The threesome went out for ice cream and a movie, and while Ted never explained who Brittany was or showed any affection, Jennifer sensed that this was more than a friend.

Ted's behavior was inappropriate and irrational. It is very harmful to insert a child into the center of a triangle. If you decide to divorce and marry a lover, careful rules must be followed (See chapter 15.) If matters are still in flux, it is cruel and confusing to divide a child's loyalties this way.

When she came in to see me, Jennifer was so upset that it took twenty minutes of comforting before she would even play. Once she settled down with the dolls and toy cars, however, she quickly blew Ted's secret. First, she took the "daddy doll" out of the dollhouse and put it in the car. "Where is Daddy going?" I asked, and then, when she didn't answer, prompted, "To visit grandma? To work?"

"I'm not supposed to tell," she said, then blurted, "Daddy is going to visit Brittany!" Next, she threw a girl doll on the floor and tucked Daddy back in the house next to the mommy doll.

It was the first time Jennifer's mother, Ann, even knew there was another woman—although she had been one of his lovers when he was still married to his first wife. Ted tried to smooth things over, saying, "Jennifer liked Brittany. Brittany is Daddy's friend," and putting the Brittany doll into the car with the father and daughter dolls.

Jennifer was having none of that, though. This time, she threw her own doll on the floor and yelled, "No! Brittany not friend of Daddy, Brittany bad for Mommy."

At my suggestion, Ann played out the scenario with the child and said, "The little girl is scared. What happened?"

After the story emerged, Ann became furious at Ted. "How could you do this to our child!" She threatened to leave, saying, "I'm not going to allow this." Ann put the mommy and Jennifer dolls in one house, and the daddy in another. Jennifer got mad and said, "Daddy wants to be with me!" She would pitch the Brittany doll across the room and say, "Daddy bad, Brittany bad, Mommy sad, Jennifer sad."

Soon, when her parents were actually living apart, Jennifer kept putting their dolls back together. "No!" she'd say, and stamp her feet.

It took many months, but eventually, when Ted and Ann witnessed the depth of their little girl's pain, they did—with the help of their own parents—reconcile for real. Had a therapist worked with them or Jennifer separately, the parents might not have united and worked as a team in order to help the child.

THE TRIANGLE GAME

If your child has overheard fights, draw a triangle with Mommy, Daddy, lover. Draw the child in the middle, but reassure the child that he/she doesn't have to choose between loving one parent or the other.

Allow the child to erase himself from inside that triangle, and draw himself next to the parents on one side. Tell your child, "I am not leaving, and you are not going to be caught in the middle anymore."

Let the child and a sibling take turns pulling on your arms, showing you exactly how it feels to be caught in a tug of war.

TELL A STORY COMBINED WITH PLAY

Stories should have a realistic moral; they should not be fantasies. If you are not reconciling, don't give false hope. If you don't know how things will end, convey that. You can't make things worse by telling stories, because the secrets are already there and they need to be brought out. (Dr. Richard Gardner developed this technique of mutual storytelling, which I used in my Family Play Therapy.)

For example, if your little one says, "The mama and the papa bear lived together happily ever after," you might add, "The mama and papa bear loved each other, but they are going to think about if they will stay in the same cabin together—the story to be continued.

"No matter what happens, though, they both love Baby Bear."

The parent or therapist should start the story to prime the pump, then have the child add on. After the child supplies his happily-ever-after moral, the adult adds the more realistic one. Give the child a reward for participating with the story.

Family Play Therapy can succeed in even the worst situations, where divorce seems inevitable.

Witness John and Sally, whom you met in the chapter on anger. He had not only punched out Sally's boss after finding her in bed with the man, but he told his kids some devastating things.

"Your mother's a whore!" he'd shouted to his daughter, Carrie, four, and his son, John, Jr., seven. "She's taking off with her boss, Scott. Mommy doesn't love you anymore, and she is going to leave you. Mommy and Daddy are going to get a divorce. Try to help Daddy to get Mommy to stop seeing Scott."

John's intention in this shocking outburst was not only revenge, but an end to the affair. He didn't consider the chaos it would cause. Carrie, four, was wetting the bed. She'd wake up screaming in the middle of the night and could barely eat. John, Jr., kept saying he was sick and refused to go to school, where he was failing his class work and misbehaving.

Their father had moved out of the house. Their mother was often out with Scott. And the two children, quite understandably, were terrified they'd be abandoned. This is the worst fear of kids, of course, since they can't take care of themselves, no matter what MacCauley Culkin says in *Home Alone*.

As a last-ditch effort, they came in for Family Play Therapy. Since the situation was so tense, I asked John to apologize to the children and explain that he was very sad and hurt and upset at Mommy, and that he didn't really mean that Mommy was bad and going to leave them. He told the kids that he loved them very much and that he and their mommy were going to try and work out their problems.

He emphasized that the problem had nothing to do with them, but that sometimes when Mommies and Daddies are lonesome, they find a friend. Sometimes when Mommies or Daddies are too busy or bossy, they find a friend like Scott. John said he had been too bossy with Mommy, and Mommy went looking for a friend. Instead of Scott, John assured the children, he would like to be Mommy's friend. And then he launched into his story.

"Once upon a time, there was a little boy and a little girl who were left all alone," John began. "Their mommy was very sad and lonely because their daddy yelled too much, drank too much, and wouldn't let her go to work. He was cross with the mommy and tried to tell the mommy what to do all the time.

" The mommy tried to talk to him, but he didn't want to listen, so one day, the mommy left to go off with another friend who wouldn't tell her what to do and who would be nice to her.

"That doesn't mean she was bad...that means the mommy was sad and the daddy still didn't know it until one night she didn't come home."

Then John, Sr., turned things over to his son. "I'd like you to go on," he said.

John, Jr., continued: "The little boy said that they liked Mommy's new friend because he bought us ice cream. He took time with us. He didn't tell us what to do. Mommy said he should be our friend and that some day he might live in the house with us."

Then Carrie chimed in: "The little girl felt bad because she liked the friend and she wasn't sure Daddy was going to like her to like Mommy's friend.

"How could she like the friend without getting Daddy mad? And if she got Daddy mad, would he still love her? Would he leave? If she didn't like the friend, then Mommy would be mad at the little girl and might leave.

"The little girl couldn't sleep because a big bear was in her room. When she told her Daddy about Mommy's friend, Daddy got mad. The little girl thought it was her fault because she was bad."

Then their father picked up the tale again. "The Daddy did not mean to take the children away from the mother. He was just upset, and the mother does not want to be away from the children...the mommy is a good mother."

It became apparent that both children were testing to see whether their parents still loved them and would stay. By forcing the adults to see and hear their pain, they allowed the whole family to do the hard work of forging forgiveness and a new life together.

In my practice, I see the child in the context of the whole family, and treat everyone together. This halts generational patterns and liberates children who would otherwise become adult children of adulterers themselves.

By unlocking those family secrets, Family Play Therapy can bring the family closer or allow members to face distance and the need to reform the relationship or to separate.

You can't run from a problem when your youngster is symptomatic. The child makes you face reality. You confront deeper issues. If you choose not to deal with them, you burden your child with a legacy that your youngster may hand down to your grandchildren. It is up to you to change their destiny.

When the Forgivable Sin Is Not Forgivable

Test Your Skills.

How much do you know about divorce? Consider the following widely held opinions:

1. Second marriages have lower divorce rates.
   False: higher

2. Adultery is lower in second marriages.
   False: higher.

3. Divorce solves a problem and gets rid of your emptiness.
   False: It gives you more emptiness for a more extended period of time.

4. It has been said that you never are really divorced when you have children.
   True.

5. Divorce is a process that starts well before you split and continues long afterward.
   True.

6. Negative ties are stronger and prevent you from letting go.
   True.
7. A divorce, like death, doesn't necessarily end a relationship.
   True.
8. It is over when it is over.
   False.
9. It takes just as long to end a relationship as it does to start one.
   True.

If you want to know about how long it takes to get over someone, factor in how many years you have been together (remember, add in years you *knew* each other). If you knew each other for two years and have been married for three to five years, if you divorce it may take at least one-and-a-half to three years to get out of the emptiness syndrome. If you are married for twenty-five years or longer, don't be alarmed if it takes a very long time to let go.

Sometimes the forgivable sin is *not* forgivable, and your only recourse is divorce. But only after real soul-searching.

BREAKING UP SHOULD BE REGARDED AS A LAST RESORT RATHER THAN AN EASY WAY OUT.

I'm distressed by the fact that, although the divorce rate has stabilized, 50 percent of today's marriages still end in divorce, and 65 percent of those have been struck by adultery. According to the National Center for Health Statistics, nearly 100,000 couples divorce each month.

I'm convinced that too often couples jettison a relationship for the wrong reasons: hurt pride, guilt, shame, denial, stubbornness. They act impulsively, just to take some sort of action out of confusion or sheer emotional exhaustion, wrongly thinking, "What else can I do?" Or they are still in denial and refuse to confront their emptiness. Divorce, in the face of all of this, may seem like an easier way out yet actually causes deeper problems.

Divorce can compound the family damage done by infidelity. According to a 1992 study by psychologist Matt McGue of the University of Minnesota, an inclination to divorce is heavily influenced by heredity—much like adultery. McGue studied the divorce rates of 1,516 pairs of twins (both identical and fraternal) and found that they rose with every family tie. If a twin's mother and father had split, for instance, the likelihood of divorce increased 10 percent; if in-laws did the same, the rate jumped to 20 percent; if a sibling did so, the rate rose another 10 percent for fraternal twins and 25 percent for identical twins.

What's more, divorce is not only disruptive but often ineffective. If you separate without coming to terms with your emptiness, you will never conquer the problems you have with intimacy. The unresolved issues will simply follow you from relationship to relationship. I see this happening extensively and expensively in divorce court, where couples are still wrestling with unresolved furies. Emotional closure shouldn't have to occur through such expensive fighting!

THINKING ABOUT DIVORCE

Yet despite all the drawbacks, it may become clear to you that ending your union is the only answer. If you have done the anger and grieving exercises in previous chapters, yet cannot bring yourself to forgive, your wounds may not be curable. You or your spouse may be unable or unwilling to make the commitment necessary to work hard at your relationship. Your relationship may be too far gone. Some people really can't go back after adultery. Something inside them dies, and they don't seek help in time.

Divorce does not signify failure. Often, it takes more courage than remaining in a bad situation. If you have sincerely tried and tried, and nothing has worked, give yourself credit for getting this far.

Amanda, for example, went to heroic lengths to save her marriage to Don, a handsome realtor who was always making passes at her friends. Then, when after four miscarriages, she at last had a healthy pregnancy, Don took up with her best friend, Sonia.

Somehow, she managed to forgive even this double betrayal. For two years after the birth of Stephen, she persevered, even though Don kept on philandering, acted jealous of the baby, and wouldn't help with childcare.

Finally, when Don refused to get help, she decided that she had too much self-worth, too much to put up with this humiliation any longer. She filed for divorce—and now her real estate career, her son, and a second marriage are all thriving.

How do you know when it is time to leave?

This is a very complex question, and one of the most difficult decisions you will ever have to make. I ask my patients to answer a series of questions to measure their true feelings before they make up their minds about divorce. I hope this "Exit Interview" will help you, too.

This is what I do with couples thinking of divorcing. **I feel very strongly that most couples divorce too hastily, and for the wrong reasons, when they really could stay together.**

Most couples fell in love but don't know how to *stay* in love. I have found that many people change their minds about divorcing, work through their emotions, and move on to forgiveness after they carefully reconsider the following questions, which I methodically go over with them before I encourage their final decision.

You should do the same. These questions could save your marriage, and 98 percent of the cases I treated saved theirs. Keep in mind the betrayed and adulterer may have different answers. **There is a very thin line between divorce and forgiveness.**

Questions to Ask Yourself When Deciding Whether or Not to Stay

1. Did you not marry for love?
2. Are you running away from emptiness?
3. Are you avoiding intimacy now that you are in the rebuilding phase? (After the affair is uncovered and stopped the real intimacy-avoiders have to look themselves in the face. That is when panic sets in.)
4. Are you a grudge-holder like other members in your family?
5. Do you have a hard time with bitterness? Do you not handle forgiveness well?
6. Did you or your partner not commit to working on your problems?
7. Is there no love left between you? *Warning: hurt numbs love.*
8. Did you receive a sexually-transmitted disease from your partner (the adulterer), which you can't forgive?
9. Are you interested only in being right so you can't forgive? Do you suffer from false pride?

10. Are you aware that negative ties are stronger and don't allow you to let go?

11. Are you confusing hurt with the death of your relationship? *Warning: Most people leave when they are hurt and don't give the other person a chance to heal themselves. This is the most common reason for divorce.*

12. Did you as the deceiver fail to work through your guilt and shame before deciding to divorce? (Many adulterers leave a marriage because of the intense guilt and shame they feel, rather than trying to work through these feelings to forgiveness.) *This is the most common cause of adulterers leaving for the wrong reason.*

13. Is the hurt too deep? Has too much time passed so you cannot forgive, yet cannot let go?

14. Is your unwillingness to work through your anger a sign you want a divorce?

15. Are you divorcing *not* because you fell in love with your new lover, but because you have unresolved guilt and it is interfering with your marriage or long-term relationship?

16. Did you use an affair specifically to get out of this relationship?

17. Do you have trouble with separation in general? Are you trying to let your partner down easy? Have you secretly always wanted to divorce?

18. Is having an affair the coward's way out? The only way you could get divorced?

19. Are you putting your lover's needs before your children's and your partner's needs?

20. Did you as the adulterer do most of the emotional work? Were you in more pain than the betrayed? Were you more willing to face the issues that drove you to the affair than your partner?

21. Are you, the betrayed, hanging onto the coattails of the betrayer, refusing to see your part, obsessing about the lover, feeling you have been

wronged? Are you using divorce as a solution to your feelings of emptiness? *This is the commonest cause of the betrayed divorcing for the wrong reason.*

22. By not taking responsibility for your part, are you making reconciliation impossible and divorce the only solution?

23. Have you failed to make the distinction between what you can do for yourself and what you need from another person?

24. Did you have an "emotional divorce" for many years?

If most of the above applies to you, perhaps divorce is the answer. However, **seek professional help before making your final decision. Remember, this is for the rest of your life! Divorce is one of the biggest steps you will ever take in your life. You have to seek every alternative you possibly can before making that decision. Don't leave yourself in a position where, after you've divorced, you find yourself saying, "If only I..."**

There are, however, some red-flag situations that must be heeded:

1. If you or the children are being subjected to emotional and physical abuse or you don't feel safe, GET OUT NOW!

2. If you or the children are becoming physically or emotionally ill, get out and seek help.

Yes, divorce can bruise children. But a study of 17,000 British families published in the June 7, 1991, issue of *Science* magazine suggests that what does most of the harm is the hostilities that existed beforehand. In the British sample—as in a similar study among 1,700 American families—half the boys developed emotional problems, and almost as many of the girls, reflecting those difficulties before the split. Make no mistake: *If a relationship is causing you and your children great pain, it may be less damaging to you all to get out.* Several studies—and my own experience—indicate that children in a family racked by conflict are better off if the parents divorce than if they stay together.

3. If you feel you need help, and your mate adamantly refuses to go along, it may be time to leave. Often, one partner initiates therapy, but the other must join in eventually if the process is to succeed. You must be patient—but you can't do it all by yourself forever.
4. If your partner is in denial, continues to cheat and lie, or won't promise not to do this again even after therapy, leave. Repeated adultery is abuse.

One woman I helped had put up with infidelities for forty-one years, claiming her husband was otherwise a good father and partner! After she came to see me, she finally realized that enough was enough, and filed for divorce—even though she swore she still loved him. He came in but refused to stop philandering, saying the affairs just felt too good and he was not hurting anyone.

5. If you feel swallowed up by a destructive relationship in which you have no rights and are treated as if you were invisible, you should leave. If the pain outweighs the pleasure, is the status quo worth preserving?

Don't be blackmailed by money, the good of the children, etc. Like Amanda, who finally divorced and made a new life for herself, you *can* survive without your adulterous mate.

6. If your partner really doesn't want you, don't stay! You can't force closeness or talk someone into loving you again. If someone tells you, "I don't love you anymore," take him/her seriously. Most times, these words are sincere. Once love dies it is over!
7. If you did not marry for love in the first place, you will most likely not stay together, there is nothing to hold you there. Some affairs, as we have noted, are motivated by a desire to head for the exit door. This is particularly true for women who married without love but lack the courage to leave until their adultery forces them out.

In some cases, a spouse will act like a dog in the manger. He doesn't want to be married to you, but he doesn't want anyone else to have you, either.

That was the case with Larry, who hadn't made love to his wife, Christina, in years though he was carrying on around town.

When Christina and the children moved out, Larry refused to support his family. He even spent a night in jail rather than comply with a court order. He kept trying to blame Christina for the situation, trying to make her feel guilty for leaving.

In therapy, she grew strong enough to admit her right to be angry. She asserted her independence, going back to school and studying computer programming while her folks minded the children. Today she is divorced, self-supporting, and proud of what she's accomplished.

If you do decide that divorce is necessary, proceed as carefully and compassionately as possible.

You may want revenge—but if you seek vengeance against your mate, you may retard your chances for future happiness with someone else, and your children's chances, too. Several studies indicate that children whose parents communicated poorly and fought unfairly were among those most likely to divorce in later life.

CHILDREN: THE SILENT WITNESSES

Children whose parents divorce because of adultery absorb a lot of guilt and take on a terrible sense of responsibility for their parents' fate.

Tammy, age five, asked, "Daddy, are you going to live with her? Don't you love Mommy and me anymore? I'll be good, I'll do my homework. I'll go to school. And I won't fight with Derrick."

She then asked her mother, in front of her father, "Mommy, are we getting a new daddy?"

The father, crying, said, "I'm never going to leave you. I'm always going to be your daddy, even if Mommy or I remarry someone else. We are both always going to love you." **Be sure to tell your children you will always love and cherish them.**

Violence

I see these hostilities reverberating through too many families. After a screaming Angela confronted Dan about his mistress, he hit her so hard, he broke her nose. Neither realized that their six-year-old daughter, Jody, had overheard the terrible fight. Suddenly, because of the trauma, she simply stopped speaking.

Meanwhile, her parents escalated their conflict to a very destructive level. On his lawyer's advice, Dan remained in the family home pending a final decree, although Angela would not cook for him, allow him into the bedroom to get his clothes, or give him his telephone messages.

They spoke only in insults—and Jody remained silent.

Finally, they brought her to me. Through Family Play Therapy, she revealed what she had witnessed, reenacting the shocking scene with toy police cars and an ambulance (both had been called during the dispute) and "Little People" dolls representing members of her family.

Her parents realized that their heedless fury was destroying them and their child. Dan realized that, if he valued his little girl more than his property, he would have to leave the house. Angela saw that she would have to let go of her animosity and find a humane way for Jody to see her daddy.

The little girl regained her speech, and the custody arrangement is working smoothly for the whole family.

Obsession

Obsession can upset children almost as much as violence can. Although she was divorced from Lester, Lil and her son, Aaron, couldn't give up the fantasy that someday he'd come crawling back.

In truth, they'd scarcely spoken in seven years. When Lester came to pick up ten-year-old Aaron, he'd honk the horn outside.

Traumatized by the stress, the boy developed severe allergies that required hospitalization. At one point, he almost died.

Concerned, his parents eventually got together to see me. In Family Play Therapy, we were able to show Lil and Lester that their "silent fighting" had to end for their son's sake. *Like all children of divorce, Aaron wanted his folks to reconcile. They did not, but they did do the next best thing, they became friends.* Aaron was elated and eventually recovered.

A FRIENDLY DIVORCE MAY BE AN OXYMORON, BUT A CIVILIZED ONE IS POSSIBLE AND ESSENTIAL, FOR THE SAKE OF THE CHILDREN.

MINIMIZING THE PAIN

To make a clean break as gently as possible you must share your pain and disappointment and anger together. (See chapter 9 for Echo, Bulletproof Vest, and Embraceable You exercises.) Cry together. Discuss the good aspects of the relationship, how you've grown, as well as issues that may arise in any new relationships. Talk about how you will tell the children. Remember: **You will need to maintain connectedness, if only for your**

**children's sake. This relationship, like any other, is fragile
and will need nurturing.**

1. *Dissipate your white-hot anger.*

    Very often, the only way couples can bring themselves to
    split is to get into a rage. Repeat the exercises in the anger,
    grief, and forgiveness chapters to solidify your *new* rela-
    tionship with your former mate even if you did them
    before reaching your decision. They will help keep the
    parting amicable and help you build your skills so that you
    can go on to a new life and a new partner with more
    dignity and less pain.

2. *Do the funeral exercise on page 147.*

    This will help you cherish and accentuate the positive
    aspects of the relationship and allow you to grieve its loss
    and let go so that a better relationship will be possible
    someday. You will have regrets and trouble with intimacy
    later on if you don't.

3. *Acknowledge how important you are to each other and how
    important your marriage has been.*

4. *Acknowledge your own part in the breakup without sinking into
    remorse or blame.*

5. *Write a letter to your spouse, but don't deliver it.*

    List what your needs and expectations were in the mar-
    riage; how your mate failed to meet them; how you yourself
    failed to go after what you wanted.

6. *If you have trouble letting go, write letters to yourself.*

    Note the appealing and not-so-appealing facets of the
    marriage and your about-to-be ex-spouse. Only after you've
    properly said goodbye to the love *and* the anger, can you
    approach intimacy with someone else.

    If eulogizing, write down negatives; if bastardizing, write
    down positives. Note both the good and the bad.

7. *If the tension and turmoil are too much, seek help with your
    children and your spouse.*

    See the same therapist together and separately to get a grip
    on your hostility before you see a divorce lawyer.

8. *Address your own needs.*

Note what was lacking in this marriage that you'll look for in your next relationship. Put it in the form of a list. Keep it somewhere handy, like your underwear or sock drawer, and consult it occasionally.

9. *Watch for symptoms in your children.* (Watch more carefully children who show *no* symptons.)

Practice Family Play Therapy with them as described in chapter 14. (Use the genogram and triangles described in earlier chapters to understand your legacy and to correct destructive patterns.)

10. *Try to make your children understand that you have done everything you could to make the marriage work.*

Remind them that both of you will continue to love them. Don't punish them or put them in the middle. **Tell them it's not their fault**.

With young children, I frequently use toy analogies (see box, below). When one parent is moving out, for instance, I note that on a paddle ball, the ball does not always come back to the same place—but it remains attached, nevertheless.

TALE OF THE TOYS

In the 2 percent of my cases where parents do divorce because of adultery, I often help them break the news to the children with parents and grandparents present.

I show them broken toys. One is a doll (or a car) that has broken in just a few pieces and can be put back together; the other is smashed to smithereens like Humpty Dumpty and cannot be mended. I let them try to glue it and then let them cry if they don't succeed.

I explain that Mommy and Daddy have been working hard to put their marriage back together, but that it proved to be too much like the second toy.

They understand, although they still feel sad. (I encourage them to grieve for the broken plaything. It's

O.K. for them to cry.) I then tell them that they will have a new relationship with their parents now, and that it will be like a new toy but it can't replace the old. It's never going to be the same; it's different. But I remind them that they often grow to like new playthings as much or even more than the old ones—although they miss the originals.

We explain that Daddy turned to a new friend, but that's not Mommy's fault. Maybe Daddy never told Mommy that she wasn't being his best friend. Maybe he didn't know how to say it.

I want them to see the equal signs as I explain that Daddy and Mommy were both very lonely and had problems, but they didn't know it for a long time. Maybe Mommy showed it by being too close to the children and not to Daddy, and Daddy by finding his new friend.

The friend didn't cause the problems...and neither did they.

11. *Don't make your children spies or marriage counselors.*

Make sure they understand that they will not be expected to defend one parent against the other or to keep secrets.

Reassure them that no matter what changes, both of you will continue to love them just as much.

Give the child permission to love both of you. Give reassurance that the child will not be rejected as disloyal if he/she meets and likes the new lover.

INTRODUCING THE NEW LOVER

When you decide that it is time for your child to meet your lover, handle the get-together with extreme care. Make sure that this develops into a sound relationship.

STEPS TO TAKE WHEN INTRODUCING A NEW LOVER:

Do not introduce the new person right away. The children need time to spend with each parent first, to assimilate the changes in the situation and rework their relationships with Mom and Dad.

Wait at least six months or longer, if possible, so that the child can grieve. Often, the lover will press for an early meeting, thinking this is a sign that marriage is in the offing. Keep the needs and feelings of your children paramount; don't give in until all of you are ready.

Do not take any action without discussing it thoroughly with your spouse first. Both must agree because if the child and spouse are not ready, it can contaminate the relationship for life between parents, child, and lover.

Lay the groundwork well. Children of any age resent meeting the third party without honest airing of feelings first. They can, in many cases, come to accept the step-parent—but not if the relationship is rushed, or the abandoned parent is not ready.

Don't nag or threaten to try and force closeness; it's counterproductive.

Don't expect anything more than decent manners. Meet on neutral turf and don't demand instant intimacy.

Greg's mistress, Polly, tried to buy the affections of his two children with gifts. Against my advice, they met three months after Greg left their mother. Daughter Tina, age four, was in the Oedipal stage where her dad could do no wrong and was therefore charmed. But Tim, age seven, was more allied with Mom and Tim refused to see Polly when she came by every week with Dad.

He was old enough to look beyond the presents and sense his mother's pain. Unfortunately, his father pressured him to love Polly because "your sister does." This only made Tim distance from his sister as well as his dad. The ill feelings continued after Greg divorced the children's mother and married Polly. This caused a split with each child allying with the opposite parent. Tina and the mother have a negative relationship now.

How to Start Over

Once you are divorced, how do you get going again? First, of course, you need time to mope and grieve (see chapter 11). But make yourself move on.

1.   Connect to support systems.

You will probably feel antisocial, but force yourself to see a lot of family friends, and take advantage of support groups such as Parents Without Partners.

2.   Forgive yourself, your partner, and your parents.

Make contact with the parent you're distant from; now is a good time to deal with the emptiness you've felt since childhood.

3.   Change your place and pace   to get a new perspective.

Take an adventure vacation, go river rafting or bicycling. Go on an archaeological dig sponsored by a museum; go somewhere you've always wanted to go—perhaps with your college alumni association.

4.   Pamper yourself at a spa or join a gym.

Exercise combats depression by releasing endorphins, the body's own feel-good medication—and it will leave you looking better, too.

5.   Find a new purpose.

Take on a new, meaningful volunteer activity. Teach reading to illiterate adults, tend to AIDS babies, work on a campaign or petition drive. It will renew your energy, make you feel good about yourself—and you might meet some great new people, as well.

6. <u>Let Go.</u>

It's over—don't clutch at negatives. After the dust clears, ask yourself: Am I still holding a grudge against my spouse? Remember, negative ties are stronger.

7. <u>Act like a single.</u>

Date. If no invitations are forthcoming, invite several pals over for dinner—and include someone you'd like to go out with. Have friends fix you up.

8. <u>Don't be afraid to be hurt again.</u>

Wisdom and change often grow out of pain. Risk and hurt are part of love. We can't love unless we put our hearts on the line. Remember, if you don't risk, loneliness is the price you pay. (Besides, now that you've mastered the skills in this book, you're better prepared!)

9. <u>Use the upheaval of divorce to make you stretch and reach out for new challenges.</u>

10. <u>Give yourself hope.</u>

Hang up a sign where you can see it every day, saying: *"I will find someone who loves me."*

The Long Way Home

Even in the nastiest of breakups, divorce doesn't have to destroy families. Consider the case of Richard and Jane.

He hit her when he found out she was having an affair; she called the police. Now they were separating and he feared that he would never see his son and daughter again because their mother would turn them against him.

I invited Richard, Jaimie, age ten, and Molly, eight, to play a "Gilligan's Island" game with me. Jane refused to participate, which made her children feel torn and disloyal about loving both parents. Eventually, I kept her in telephone touch with the feelings her kids were expressing.

In Family Play Therapy, the children's feelings of being torn, disloyal, and forced into a triangle with their parents came through. They wanted to visit their father, whom they loved, but they were afraid they would be punished by their mother. They needed their mother very much. Who would take care of them if she got mad since their father was already gone? Jaimie started the storytelling based on the "Gilligan" game.

"The father's out there on the island," he declared.

"Does he like it out there?" I asked.

"Nah—nobody likes him."

"A coconut fell on his head, " Molly chimed in.

"He's hurt," said their father, Richard.

"So who cares?" shrugged Jaimie.

"I care. He might be dead," Molly whimpered.

"Where's everybody else?" I asked.

"The boy and girl are over here in a house," Jaimie replied. "So's the mother. She won't let them help the father."

"Why not?"

"He did a real bad thing and he had to be punished," Jaimie said.

"The island is the father's jail?" I asked.

"Yeah."

"People get visitors in jail," their father suggested.

"The girl could bring him food and water," Molly said. (Molly was open about the affection she felt for her father and then admitted she was the little girl in the story.)

"The father would like that," said Richard, his voice cracking with emotion.

"What would the mother do?" I asked.

"She'd be very mad," admitted Molly. "Maybe kick the girl onto the island, too. But the girl doesn't care."

"The little boy and the little girl can't get to the island anyway," Jaimie said. "They can't drive the boat."

Sensing Jaimie's fear that he had no power to maintain contact, I suggested that the father could be happy on the island because there was a nice beach and friendly animals and that he could drive the boat to the house and get the children to enjoy "Gilligan's Island" with him.

At that point, Richard broke down and cried, apologizing profusely for hitting their mother. I suggested that when people do bad things, they do not have to be punished forever. I suggested that forgiving people for the bad things that they do was also important. "Even God makes mistakes," I said.

After giving Jaimie *my* permission to love and visit his father, I told Jaimie to also ask his mother's permission to love and visit his father *in the game*. He did so with a little coaching from me, and she relented in *real life*. Jaimie also worked out his ambivalence by observing Molly's positive response to her father in the game.

Eventually, through the testimony of an innocent child, the family found that their love outweighed their bitterness.

Their rapprochement lessened the odds that Molly and Jaimie or their children and grandchildren will have to live out their dangerous legacy. By working together to understand and forgive after adultery and divorce, this family bettered their children's chance for happiness.

By reading this book, so have you.

Is Your Choice of Divorce Really Your Fear of Reconciliation?

How you and your partner answer the next questions, how much effort you are willing to put in, will decide reconciliation or divorce.

These types of questions have to be asked of yourself and your partner before you can make any definite decision about divorce or reconciliation. If there are more yes's than no's you may be divorcing for the wrong reasons. If there are more no's than yes's, your marriage probably can be saved, so work harder.

1. Are you leaving mainly because you can't deal with the uncertainty any longer?

2. Are you leaving because of impulsiveness?
3. Are you leaving because you just want to take any action even if it is not the right action?
4. Are you leaving because of confusion or hurt?
5. Are you leaving mainly because of pessimism?
6. Are you leaving because of emotional exhaustion?
7. Are you leaving mainly because the hurt has numbed your love?
8. Do you feel not in love anymore, even though you fell in love once and you married for love?
9. Are you leaving mainly due to stubbornness, which is preventing you from rebuilding and reconciling?
10. Is your indecisiveness—not knowing who to choose—causing you to leave those whom you love?
11. Are you provoking your lover or your partner into making the decision to get out of this turmoil? Are you forcing divorce?
12. Are you leaving mainly because your partner refuses professional help? Are you aware that sometimes the *runaway* is slow to come around and you, the pursuer, need to lead?
13. Do you see that divorce doesn't solve your problem?
14. Do you feel blame gives you more control and you can't get beyond this?
15. Are you leaving mainly because you believe getting rid of a person is getting rid of your problem?
16. Are you divorcing before you have a *conscious* awareness of your emptiness, your partner's and your parents'?
17. Have you gone through the pain together now to avoid greater pain later whether you stay or leave?

18. Do you understand why it happened? Can you be sad together as you prepare to leave?
19. Do you understand the fragile nature of relationships and the skills necessary to do it differently?
20. Will you take this second chance either with your partner or someone new and do it differently?
21. Do you know divorce doesn't always end a relationship, especially if you have children?
22. Have you discussed divorce with your children?

Some Pertinent Questions

FOR THE BETRAYER:

1. Is indecisiveness causing you to lose or leave those you love?
2. Are you still in denial? Do you feel you are not hurting anyone with your adulterous behavior?
3. Have you forgiven the betrayed and yourself?
4. Do you still idealize or eulogize the lover?

FOR THE BETRAYED:

1. Are you leaving because of the adulterer's denial and unwillingness to stop the affair (most common and acceptable reason for divorce)?
2. Have you forgiven the adulterer and yourself?

FOR BOTH:

Is the selfish part of you still having trouble? Are you still unable to block out your own hurt and righteous thoughts, instead of empathizing with your partner by listening and validating?

• 16 •

Adultery: The Forgivable Sin

The life which is unexamined is not worth living.
                                                    --PLATO

Those who cannot remember the past are condemned to
repeat it.
                                          —George Santayana

I know that adultery does not always have to have a tragic
ending. I know it not only because of my experience with
hundreds of patients, but because of what happened to my
parents, my husband, and myself.

By now, I hope you know it, too.

Today, my parents have found Real-Life Love, and they are
enjoying the most rewarding relationships of their lives—
with each other, and with my brother and myself.

We have made peace with those who caused us pain, and
we have hammered out connections: me with my father, my
father with his mother, my mother with her late father (at the
graveside). And I have finally defeated my anxieties and
dared to seize incredible happiness with my second husband,
Jeff—who has conquered some fears of his own.

It wasn't easy for me to renounce my legacy of fear and mistrust. Without realizing it, I went into denial and workaholic retreat for nearly twenty years after my divorce. Then I met Jeff, a very intelligent and handsome periodontist. He had also been long divorced from his first spouse, and had just been hurt again when a yearlong relationship fell apart.

We had an immediate rapport. After three months of dating, I summoned my courage and asked what our prospects were.

"Are we dating each other exclusively, or are we seeing others as well?" I asked, trying to fend off my fear of betrayal as well as my desire to avoid getting trapped in a triangle.

"No," he answered, saying just the words I wanted to hear. "I am happy with you. I don't want to date anyone else."

Still, the nagging doubts persisted. "Can I trust him? Will he be like my father? Will he hurt me, too?"

I should have suspected that trouble was brewing when we planned our first vacation together. I wanted to go on a romantic trip to the Caribbean, but Jeff balked. That destination sounded too much like a honeymoon spot to him—why not Cape Cod, instead? I, being a typical pursuer, thought, "What's wrong with a honeymoon?" He, a typical runaway, decided—without telling me—it was time to date other women. He answered a personal ad in a magazine, which was how *we* had met.

With just a little lobbying, I convinced him to go to the Caribbean, where we had a glorious time. That was where we fell in love...or so I thought. Not long after we returned, however, I answered the phone at his apartment one day and took a message from a woman who was calling to confirm a date.

It was a week before I was supposed to meet his mom, and he had panicked.

I was devastated. I had known that someday my illicit legacy would reassert itself if and when I allowed myself to love again; and now it had indeed hit—hard. All the

hurt, rage, and fear over my father's adultery washed over me as strongly as it had at age seven. I felt like my mother must have. I told him the relationship was over. Even though we were not married, we were committed to each other. He had broken an intensely serious promise. Even if he didn't take the promise literally, this constituted infidelity in my eyes.

Jeff pleaded with me to hear him out. He had not been *physically* unfaithful, he assured me, and he did not even understand his own behavior.

"It is not like me. I just feel very strange inside. I was not trying to hurt you. I don't know why I did it. I can't lose you. I think I'm falling in love with you. I love you," he declared.

I was too upset and hurt to listen. Becoming a runaway myself, I fled from my own fear—the fear of being betrayed because I'd made a commitment. I hid behind Jeff, classifying him as the villain and me the blameless victim, even though I knew we were both acting out similar deep-seated fears.

Finally, I called up the one man I had learned to forgive and trust after all our years of soul-searching work together—my father—and asked for his advice.

"Bonnie," he said, "no one should know better than you that relationships are hard work. Before you leave Jeff, find out if he was scared. Was Jeff's action a cry for help, as it was for me?"

Yes, as it turned out, it was. Once I agreed to hear him out, thanks to Dad's intervention, I learned that Jeff was still afraid of closeness. Sadly, his father had died suddenly when he was only twenty-two, before he had finished dental school; his first marriage had broken up. He had bottled up his sense of betrayal and fear of abandonment. Now he was falling in love. He was afraid that he would make a mistake again, having married the first time to ease his emptiness. He was also terrified that I would leave suddenly, as his father had. He had distanced himself to reduce his involvement and protect his vulnerability.

He did not have a sexual affair, but he did send out a signal, a cry for help—just as my father had said.

I was a therapist. I listen to other people's problems. Why didn't I listen to Jeff's? Because, at the time, this was still the unforgivable sin to me. Even though I'd helped my parents find forgiveness, I still couldn't find it in myself.

Then my father returned the favor and helped me as I had helped him. He made up for the lost time when he wasn't there for me by being there for me now, and for Jeff.

He enabled us to see how much we meant to each other, and to know that the relationship was worth every effort we could make.

First, as Dr. Fogarty had taught us to do, my father accompanied Jeff to his father's grave so he could reconnect and try to ease his feeling of betrayal and abandonment. Jeff had never cried for his father; now, he cried for him with mine.

It turned out that, wanting to shield him from the tragedy so that he would continue in dental school, his mother had not told him his father had cancer. Jeff had thought they had all the time in the world together, so the sudden death was a shattering blow.

My dad spoke first. "Your son here loves you so and is so distraught that you're not here to help him at another important crossroad in his life. I know you would be proud of him today. He wants to marry Bonnie, but he is having difficulty showing his deeper feelings. Part of it is your death, part of it is that he married his first wife to avoid the emptiness of your death. Instead, he felt even emptier and had to leave her.

"Jeff needs to talk to you, and I will take your place and help him if it's okay with you. I know he loves her like I loved my wife, but I too had trouble showing it until I lost her. He could lose Bonnie if he doesn't come to terms with his fears because of your death."

Then he hugged a shaking Jeff, who spoke: "Dad, I have a deep hole, a deep void, something stops me from committing myself all the way to Bonnie. I love you. I need you and your blessings so I won't make the same mistake. Saying I love you and miss you and crying with my new dad holding me helps me.

"I need to forgive Mom—she did her best. She never told me you were dying, but she was in her own pain." Jeff began to draw closer to all of us soon after this. With my father's support, he forgave his father for leaving and himself for not saying goodbye. He forgave his wonderful mother for trying to protect him. She also enabled Jeff to grieve the loss by reminding him of how special he had been to his father, who was not a demonstrative man. She encouraged him to trust again—so that he could finally let himself love me.

A few months later, Jeff called my dad and said, "Dad, I love you. Is it alright for me to be in the family as a son? I love your daughter. I feel passion and friendship. I know we'll be happy and she will help me communicate and ask for what I need." My father, crying, replied, "I now have not one son but two."

That was five years ago. Although we were sharing and enjoying closeness, we were secretly fearful of it. Today, my husband and I turn to each other for healing. He learned to face his fears rather than flee, and helped me to face mine, too.

Jeff came to appreciate how much I meant to him, as my father finally appreciated how important my mother was to him. Had I not worked on my relationship with my father, I might have mistaken Jeff's natural fear of intimacy for a predisposition to adultery.

Fidelity was and is just as important to him as to me. It is my experience that couples who discuss fidelity before marriage are likelier to observe it afterward.

We dealt with our problems together as my parents had done. I saw that I could handle abandonment if it happened without collapsing. Jeff realized he could care for someone without losing his freedom or being left.

I still have occasional nightmares of being abandoned by my husband and my father—especially while I was writing this book. This is not unusual, it is the remnant of a legacy of a family pattern of betrayal. The difference is that now I can share these bad dreams with the two men in my life—and feel very loved, comforted, and secure.

My mother and father's favorite song is "You Always Hurt the One You Love." I know how true it is.

We always inflict pain on the ones we care most about, because our expectations are so high. Our parents hurt us, our spouse hurts us, we hurt our kids. But as we come to understand that hurt is an inevitable part of love, we can heal. Hurt should be shared for healing.

Many of those who commit adultery are trying to ease an enormous ache—an ache that was passed down to them from their parents. Some families try to deaden this painful emptiness with alcohol, divorce, or overwork, and a great many with infidelity.

If you can understand those realities about adultery, you will not find yourself forced to repeat or retreat. Indeed, like a recovering alcoholic, you may discover a new joy in life and develop a new sensitivity to others.

If you can reach the point of forgiveness, you will free yourself—and your children—from this multigenerational tragedy.

I am no longer cowering under the covers. I have stepped into the light—and I hope that this book will help bring you there, too.

In closing, I think of another of my mother's favorite sayings, Alexander Pope's famous dictum: "To err is human, to forgive, divine." I believe that forgiveness is very human, too. I offer to you the experiences of my parents, my partner, and myself, as well as of my patients, as evidence that "the unforgivable sin" is forgivable indeed.

And now I'd like to share with you the letters that my parents and I wrote to each other as part of our forgiveness exercise.

May they inspire you to achieve as much happiness as we have found.

As Mom says, Love really *can* conquer all.

Dear Bon,

I love you and I've tried to show you and make up for my immaturity, mistakes. I have so many regrets. I am thankful for your and Mom's confidence in me.

I love you,

Dad

Dear Mom,

In my high-school year book you wrote, "Someday life will take you on different paths of both good and bad. You can't be on one without finding yourself on the other, but if you have courage and stick with your beliefs, you will find the way back."

You helped me to understand human behavior, encouraged me in my dream to help others. I thank you for having the courage to allow me to share our pain and joy with others with this book so they may find their way as they walk those paths.

I love you for standing by Dad when he needed you, and leaving him when he needed to see the damage he was doing, and "the wisdom to know the difference." Thanks for always being my friend, and showing me the way to help the couples, individuals, and children I see in my practice. It has been your optimism, faith, and hope that have inspired me with my patients.

I love you,

Your Princess

Dear Dad,

I am sorry that I was not there for you and shunned you. I was ashamed of you because I did not understand, and I was too scared to tell you. I did not know we had the same pain.

I hope this book not only shows our family's courage but helps take the stigma out of the word "adultery" and gives hope to those facing this "unforgivable sin." I offer my legacy not to condone affairs, but so others may see that they are a cry for help.

A new bond can be formed and a couple can grow from this symptom to learn trust and respect. You taught me that fidelity is a responsibility, a trust, a bond that can be fragile but repairable.

You taught me about forgiveness. For this I thank you. For this I love you. Thanks, Dad, for the new legacy of the forgivable sin.

I am proud you are my father.

I am proud to be your daughter.

You taught me how to love and grow!

> I love you,
> your loving princess,
>
> Bonnie

To My Wife and Daughter,

I am happy you both forgave me for all the hurt I caused you, but as you know, my compulsion made me do the things I am not proud of.

I want to especially thank you, Bonnie, for making sure I got the professional help I needed.

I am now a happily married man and making up for lost time by doing things that make my family and me happy.

I thank God for giving me the strength to overcome my sickness.

Love forever,

Your husband and father

Princess Dear,

I am so proud of the wonderful work you are doing, and all through your life you have always wanted to help someone. Most of all, you helped me! I felt trapped, unloved, unhappy, and thought there was no place to turn. Bon, you made sure I got help through therapy and I have never been sorry.

I put aside my pride (which I thought was important). But what was important was my love for Dad—and I really think it is true "love conquers all." If you both work at it. Thank you, sweetheart, all your knowledge, schooling, and perseverance came to the rescue of your own family.

I have never been happier than I am today. In our Golden Years, Dad and I are not alone. We take care of each other and are enjoying each other's company. I am so full of love for you, Brother, and Dad. I wake up each morning and thank God how happy I am now.

All my love,

Mom

To the Readers,

Help is available to the people who want it. We were helped through therapy because we wanted it! And we worked at it! And you can do the same. Don't be afraid to seek professional help. Your days will be brighter and you will be able to laugh more than you have in a long while. It is wonderful to be able to cope with your life finally and make the changes that are needed through therapy.

We did it and you can too!

Sincerely,

Hy and Paula Eaker

Bibliography

Anthony, E. J. *The Family and the Psychoanalytic Process in Children. "The Psychoanalytic Study of the Child,"* vol. 35. New Haven: Yale University Press, 1980.

Bach, G. R. and Wyden, P. *The Intimate Enemy: How to Fight Fair in Love and Marriage.* New York: William Morrow & Co., 1968.

Bader, Ellyn, and Pearson, Peter T. *In Quest of the Mythical Mate: A Developmental Approach to Diagnosis and Treatment in Couples Therapy.* New York: Brunner/Mazel, 1988.

Barbach, Lonnie, and Geisinger, David L. *Going the Distance: Secrets to Lifelong Love.* New York: Doubleday, 1991.

Bartocci, Barbara. "When He's Unfaithful: How Some Women Cope." *McCall's,* May 1989, p. 49.

Bevando Sobal, Barbara. "Nice People Get Sexually Transmitted Diseases." *Matrimonial Law Monthly,* vol. II, no. 3 March 1991, p. 3.

"Births, Marriages, Divorces, and Death for January 1991." *Monthly Vital Statistics Report,* p. 3.

Borger, Gloria. "Private Lives, Public Figures." *U.S. News & World Report,* 18 May, 1987, p. 20.

Botwin, Carol. "Wander Lust: What Kind of Man Cheats on His Wife?" *Redbook,* October 1988, p. 118.

Botwin, Carol. *Men Who Can't Be Faithful: How to Pick Up the Pieces When He's Breaking Your Heart.* New York: Warner Books, 1988.

Bowen, M. "Toward a Differentiation of Self in One's Own Family of Origin. In *Georgetown Symposium Papers, I,* edited by I. Fandres and J. Lorio. Washington, D.C.: Georgetown University Press, 1976.

Bowen, Murray. *Family Therapy in Clinical Practice.* New York: J. Aronson, 1978.

Bradshaw, John. *Creating Love: The Next Great Stage of Growth*. New York: Bantam Books, 1992.

Bradshaw, John. *Homecoming*. New York: Bantam Books, 1990.

Bradshaw, John. *Bradshaw on The Family*. New York: Health Communications, 1987.

Broderick, Carlfred. *Couples: How to Confront Problems and Maintain Loving Relationships*. New York: Simon and Schuster, 1979.

Brody, Jane. "A New Look at Children and Divorce." The *New York Times*. June 7, 1991, p. C1.

Brown, Emily M. *Patterns of Infidelity and Their Treatment, Frontiers in Couples and Family Therapy*, no. 3. New York: Brunner/Mazel, 1991.

Brzeczek, Richard and Elizabeth; DeVita, Sharon. *Addicted to Adultery: How We Saved Our Marriage/How You Can Save Yours*. New York: Bantam Books, 1989.

Carter, E., and Orfanidis, M. M. "Family Therapy with the Therapist's Family of Origin." In *Family Therapy in Clinical Practice*, edited by M. Bowen. New York: Gardner Press, 1978.

DeAngelis, Barbara. *Are You the One for Me?* New York: Doubleday, 1992.

Delis, Dean C. with Phillips, Cassandra. *The Passion Paradox: Patterns of Love and Power in Intimate Relationships*. New York: Bantam Books, 1990.

Dolesh, Daniel J. and Lehman, Sherelynn. *Love Me, Love Me Not: How to Survive Infidelity*. New York: PaperJacks, 1985.

Eaker, Bonnie. "Unlocking the Family Secret in Family Play Therapy," *Child and Adolescent Social Work*. vol. 3 no. 4, Human Sciences Press. (Winter 1986).

The Family Therapy Networker, vol. 13 no. 3. (May/June 1989).

Fogarty, Thomas F. *The Distancer and the Pursuer*. Compendium II, The Best of the Family. New Rochelle, New York: The Center for Family Learning, 1978–1983.

————. *Fusion*. Compendium I, The Best of the Family. Rye Brook, New York: The Center for Family Learning, and Family Center Georgetown University Medical Center, Washington, D.C., 1973–1978.

————. *On Emptiness and Closeness—Part I and Part II*. Compendium I, The Best of the Family. Rye Brook, New York: The Center for Family Learning, and Family Center Georgetown University Medical Center, Washington, D.C., 1973–1978.

————. *On Love, Respect and Connectedness: An Analysis*. Compendium III, The Best of the Family. Rye Brook, New York: The Center for Family Learning, 1984–1992.

————. *Operating Principles I, II, and III*. Compendium II, The Best of the Family. New Rochelle, New York: The Center for Family Learning, 1978–1983.

————. "System, Concepts, and Dimensions of Self." In *Family Therapy*, edited by P. Guerin. New York: Gardner Press, 1976.

————. *Thoughts on Divorce*. Compendium I, The Best of the Family. Rye Brook, New York: The Center for Family Learning, and Family Center Georgetown University Medical Center, Washington, D.C., 1973–1978.

_____. *Thoughts on the Extended Family.* Compendium III, The Best of the Family. Rye Brook, New York: The Center for Family Learning, 1984–1992.

_____. *Triangles.* Compendium I, The Best of the Family. Rye Brook, New York: The Center for Family Learning, and Family Center Georgetown University Medical Center, Washington, D.C., 1973–1978.

Fraiberg, Selma.*The Magic Years.* New York: Charles Scribner, 1959.

Gardner, Richard A. *Psychotherapeutic Approaches to the Resistant Child.* New York: J. Aronson, 1975.

_____. *Psychotherapeutic Techniques of Richard A. Gardner.* New York: J. Aronson, 1988.

_____. *Psychotherapy With Children of Divorce.* New York: J. Aronson, 1976.

_____. *Therapeutic Communication With Children: The Mutual Story-Telling Technique.* New York: Sciences House, 1971.

_____. *Understanding Children: A Parent's Guide to Child Rearing.* Cresskill, New Jersey: Creative Therapeutics, 1979.

Garmezy, N., and Rutter, M. *Stress, Coping and Development in Children.* New York: McGraw Hill, 1983.

Ginsberg, B. "Parents as Therapeutic Agents: The Usefulness of Filial Therapy in a Community Mental Health Center," *American Journal of Community Psychology,* vol. 4 no. 1 (1976): 47–54.

Golden, Gail, and Hill, M. "A Token of Loving: From Melancholia to Mourning." *Clinical Social Work Journal* vol. 19 (Spring 1991): p. 23.

Gordon, Barbara. *Jennifer Fever: Older Men, Younger Women.* New York: Harper & Row, 1988.

Gordon, Lori Heyman. *PAIRS Handbook: The Practical Application of Intimate Relationship Skills.* Falls Church, Virginia: PAIRS Foundation, 1989.

_____. *PAIRS Therapist Training Manual and Curriculum Guide.* Falls Church, Virginia: PAIRS Foundation, 1990.

_____. *PAIRS Workshop.* Falls Church, Virginia: PAIRS Foundation, 1989 and 1990.

Gray, John. *Men Are From Mars, Women Are From Venus.* New York: Harper Collins, 1992.

Greely, Andrew. *Faithful Attraction.* New York: Tor Books, 1990.

Guerin, Philip J., Jr., and Fay, Leo F. *Triangles in Marital Conflict.* Compendium III, The Best of the Family. Rye Brook, New York: The Center for Family Learning, 1984–1992.

Guerin, Philip J., Jr., and Gordon, Edward M. *Triangles, Trees and Temperament in the Child Centered Family.* Compendium II. New Rochelle, New York: The Center for Family Learning, 1978–1983.

Guerin, Philip J., Jr., Fay, L., Burden, S. L., and Kautto, J. G. *The Evaluation and Treatment of Marital Conflict: A Four Stage Approach.* New York: Basic Books, 1987.

Guerin, Philip, J., Jr. *Family Therapy: Theory and Practice.* New York: Gardner Press, 1976.

Gurman, A. S.; Knishern, D. P.; and Pinsof, W. M. "Research on the

Process and Outcome of Marital Family Therapy." In *Handbook of Psychotherapy and Behavior Change*, 3rd ed., edited by S. L. Garfield and A. E. Bergin. New York: John Wiley, 1986.

Haley, J. and Hoffman, L. *Techniques of Family Therapy*. New York: Basic Books, 1967.

Hall, Trish. "Breaking Up Is Becoming Harder to Do." The *New York Times* 14 March, 1991, p. C1.

Hendrix, Harville. *Getting the Love You Want: A Guide for Couples*. New York: Henry Holt, 1988.

_____. *Couples Workshop Manual: A Couples Study Guide for IMAGO Relationship Therapy*. New York: The Institute for Relationship Therapy, 1990.

_____. *A Therapist's Guide to the Couples Therapy Manual*. New York: The Institute for Relationship Therapy, 1991.

_____. *IMAGO Relationship Therapy: A Workshop for Couples*. New York: The Institute for Relationship Therapy, 1991.

_____. *Keeping the Love You Find: A Workshop for Singles*. New York: Institute for Relationship Therapy, 1992.

_____. *Keeping the Love You Find: A Guide for Singles*. New York: Pocket Books, 1992.

_____. *Keeping the Love You Find*. Lecture. New York: Institute for Relationship Therapy, 1991.

_____. *Keeping the Love You Find*. Workbook, IMAGO Relationship Therapy. New York: Institute for Relationship Therapy, 1991.

"How to Find a Marriage Therapist." *Bride's*, December 1989–January 1990, p. 134.

"Intimacy After Cancer." *News Report*, University of Texas MD Anderson Cancer Center, Houston, Texas, 8 May, 1991.

Kaplan, Helen Singer. "The Two Real Reasons Husbands Have Affairs." *Redbook*, June 1984, p. 20.

Karpel, M. A. "Family Secrets." *Family Process* 19 (1980): 295–306.

Kiley, Dan.*What To Do When He Won't Change: Getting What You Need From the Man You Love*. New York: G. P. Putnam, 1987.

Klein, M. "The Psychoanalytic Play Technique." In *The Therapeutic Use of Child's Play*, edited by C. Schaefer. New York: Jason Aronson, 1981.

Krantzler, Mel. *Creative Divorce: A New Opportunity for Personal Growth*. New York: New American Library, 1975.

Kutner, Lawrence. "Telling Children That You Are Divorcing," *The New York Times*. 21 March, 1991, p. C1.

Latici, Elena. "Will He Love Your Kids?" *New Woman*, May 1988, p. 62.

Lawson, Annette. *Adultery: An Analysis of Love and Betrayal*. New York: Basic Books, 1988.

Lazarus, A. *The Practice of Multimodal Therapy*. Baltimore: The Johns Hopkins University Press, 1981.

Leigh, Julia Hood. "Is Monogamy a Myth?" *Health*, February 1990, p. 66.

Lerner, Harriet Goldhor. *The Dance of Anger: A Woman's Guide to Changing the Patterns of Intimate Relationships*. New York: Harper & Row, 1985.

_____. *The Dance of Intimacy: A Women's Guide to Courageous Acts of Change in Key Relationships*. New York: Harper & Row, 1989.

Lieberman, Florence. *Social Work With Children*. New York: Human Sciences, 1979.

Love, Patricia, with Jo Robinson. *The Emotional Incest Syndrome: What to Do When a Parent's Love Rules Your Life*. New York: Bantam Books, 1990.

"Marital Instability Grows: Most Recent Marriages in U.S. Are Likely to Fail," *Family Planning Perspectives*, p. 234.

McAdams, Dan P. *Intimacy: The Need to Be Close. How the Need for Intimacy Influences Our Relationships, Life, Choices, and Sense of Identity*. New York: Doubleday, 1989.

Melinkoff, Ellen, and Giler, Janet. "Infidelity in the '80s: The Steamy Facts." *Cosmopolitan*, November 1988, p. 226.

Mithers, Carol Lynn. "Lust in Your Heart: At What Point Does a Fantasy About Someone Become Infidelity?" *Glamour*, October 1987, p. 304.

Moultrup, David J. *Husbands, Wives & Lovers: The Emotional System of the Extramarital Affair*. New York: The Guilford Press, 1990.

Nadelson, C., Polonsky, D., and Mathews, M. A. "Marriage as a Developmental Process." In *Marriage and Divorce: A Contemporary Perspective*, edited by C. Nadelson and D. Polonsky. New York/London: The Guildford Press, 1984.

Napier, Augustus Y. *The Fragile Bond: In Search of an Equal, Intimate and Enduring Marriage*. New York: Harper & Row, 1988.

_____, with Whitaker, Carl. *The Family Crucible: The Intense Experience of Family Therapy*. New York: Harper & Row Publishers, 1978.

Norman, P. G. "Operational Mourning and Its Role in Conjoint Family Therapy." *Community Mental Health Journal* 1(4), 1965.

O'Neill, George, and O'Neill, Nena. *Open Marriage: A New Life Style for Couples*. New York: M. Evans, 1972.

Penney, Alexandra. *How to Keep Your Man Monogamous*. New York: Bantam Books, 1989.

Pietropinto, Anthony, and Simenauer, Jacqueline. *Husbands and Wives: Nationwide Survey of Marriage*. New York: Times Books, 1979.

Pincus, L., and Dare, C. *Secrets in the Family*. New York: Pantheon, 1978.

Pittman, Frank. *Private Lies: Infidelity and the Betrayal of Intimacy*. New York: W. W. Norton, 1990.

Powell, John. *The Secret of Staying in Love: Loving Relationships Through Communication*. Allen, Texas: Tabor, 1974.

Rhodes, Sonya, with Susan Schneider. *Second Honeymoon: A Pioneering Guide for Reviving the Mid-Life Marriage*. New York: William Morrow, 1992.

Richardson, Laurel. *The New Other Woman: Contemporary Single Women in Affairs With Married Men*. New York: Free Press, 1985.

Rubin, Lillian B. *Intimate Strangers: Men and Women Together*. New York: Harper & Row, 1983.

Safer, D. "Conjoint Play Therapy for the Young Child and His Parents." *Archives of General Psychiatry* 13 (1965): 320–326.

Sager, C. J. *Marriage Contracts and Couples Therapy*. New York: Free Press, 1976.

Scarf, M. *Intimate Partners: Patterns in Love and Marriage*. New York: Ballantine, 1987.

Schaefer, C., ed. *The Therapeutic Use of Child's Play*. New York: J. Aronson, 1981.

Schneider, Jennifer P. *Back From Betrayal: A Ground-Breaking Guide to Recovery for Women Involved With Sex-Addicted Men*. New York: Ballantine Books, 1988.

_____, and Schneider, Burt. *Sex, Lies and Forgiveness: Couples Speaking Out on Healing From Sex Addiction*. Hazelden Foundation, 1991.

Sills, Judith. *A Fine Romance: The Psychology of Successful Courtship—Making It Work for You*. Los Angeles: Jeremy P. Tarcher, 1987.

Tannen, Deborah. *That's Not What I Meant:How Conversational Style Makes or Breaks Relationships*. New York: Ballantine, 1986.

_____. *You Just Don't Understand: Women and Men in Conversation*. New York: William Morrow, 1990.

Thomas, A., Chess, S., and Birch, H. G. *Temperament and Behavior Disorders in Children*. New York: New York University Press, 1968.

Toufexis, Anastasia. "Sex Lives and Videotape." *Time Magazine*, 29 October, 1990, p. 104.

Thompson, Anthony. "Extramarital Sex: A Review of the Research Literature." *The Journal of Sex Research*, 19 (February 1983): 1–22.

"Unfaithfully Yours: Adultery in America." *People*, p. 85.

Vaughan, Peggy. *The Monogamy Myth: A New Understanding of Affairs and How to Survive Them*. New York: New Market Press, 1989.

Vaughn, Diane. *Uncoupling: How Relationships Come Apart*. New York: Vintage Books, 1987.

Viscott, David. *I Love You, Let's Work It Out*. New York: Pocket Books, 1987.

Watzlawick, P., Beavin, J., and Jackson, D. D. *Pragmatics of Human Communication: A Study of Interactional Patterns, Pathologies, and Paradoxes*. New York: W. W. Norton, 1967.

Westen, Robin. "My Father's Affair: How It Changed the Whole Family." *Glamour*, November 1985, p. 105.

Whitfield, Charles L. *Healing the Child Within: Discovery and Recovery for Adult Children of Dysfunctional Families*. Deerfield Beach, Florida: Health Communications, 1987.

Williamson, Marianne. *A Return to Love: Reflections on the Principles of a Course in Miracles*. New York: Harper Collins, 1992.

Winnicott, D. W. *Playing and Reality*. New York: Penguin, 1980.

Wolfe, Linda. *Playing Around: Women and Extramarital Sex*. New York: New American Library, 1976.